W9-CNA-540

Quick
WEEKNIGHT
DINNERS *for Two*

Ranch-Style Shrimp (p. 177) and Corn with Poblano and Cream (p. 178)

Quick
WEEKNIGHT
DINNERS *for Two*

American Express Publishing Corporation
New York

FOOD & WINE MAGAZINE
Editor in Chief: Dana Cowin
Creative Director: Stephen Scoble
Food Editor: Tina Ujlaki

FOOD & WINE BOOKS
Editor in Chief: Judith Hill
Art Director: Nina Scerbo
Managing Editor: Terri Mauro
Copy Editor: Barbara Mateer
Editorial Assistant: Evette Manners
Production Manager: Yvette Williams-Braxton

Vice President, Consumer Marketing: Mark V. Stanich
Vice President, Books and Information Services: John Stoops
Marketing Director: Thomas Reynolds
Operations Manager: Doreen Camardi
Business Manager: Joanne Ragazzo

PRODUCED BY BSM GROUP, LLC, NEW YORK CITY
Project Manager: Scott Mowbray
Art Director: Rick Staehling
Food Editor: Susan Stuck
Managing Editor: Terri Brandmueller
Wine Consultant: Wayne Young

COVER PHOTO: **Elizabeth Watt**
Food Stylist: Dora Jonassen   Prop Stylist: Randi Barritt
BACK COVER PHOTOS: **Elizabeth Watt, Ann Stratton**
Top row, left to right: Grilled Tuna and Salad, page 110; Chicken in a Bun, page 205
Middle row, left to right: Pan Frying Secret, page 124; Hot Soup Night, page 228
Bottom row, left to right: Fast Moroccan Feast, page 154; BLT Update, page 117

AMERICAN EXPRESS PUBLISHING CORPORATION
©1998 American Express Publishing Corporation

Library of Congress Catalog Card Number:
Quick weeknight dinners for two.
p. cm.
Includes bibliographical references and index.
ISBN 0916103-42-0
1. Dinners and dining. 2. Cookery for two. 3. Quick and easy cookery. 4. Menus.   I. Food & wine (New York, N.Y.)
TX737.Q53   1998
641.641.5'61—dc21
97-46537
CIP

Published by American Express Publishing Corporation
1120 Avenue of the Americas, New York, New York 10036
Manufactured in the United States of America

INTRODUCTION

All editors love to talk to their readers. Such conversations allow for the type of unscientific research that can yield genuinely useful information. In our case, we always ask the readers we meet what they have cooked from issues of FOOD & WINE Magazine or from our books. We have found that most people go for speed. Recipes from the fast-cooking department in the magazine rate high because everyone likes the blend of quick ideas and big flavors.

A surprise finding from our encounters with readers, backed up by surveys of those who buy our books, is that the majority of you cook for two most of the time. So we decided to put together this collection, dedicated to couples, from menus that have appeared in the popular fast-cooking column.

Many of the ingredients for these recipes are sitting on your pantry shelf waiting for a call to action. And you can find the necessary fresh ingredients easily. The dishes in each menu require very little preparation or cooking time, and the result is a meal that's simple to make for two . . . and simply delicious.

Editor in Chief
FOOD & WINE Magazine

Editor in Chief
FOOD & WINE Books

CONTENTS

Spring

Summer

Fall

Winter

Pappardelle with Olives, Thyme, and Lemon (p. 239) and Quick Winter Ratatouille (p. 240)

Pairing Wine with Weeknight Dinners

Pairing food and wine has often been made out to be mysterious, and I suspect that this mystery is one of the reasons Americans lag behind Europeans in wine consumption—we simply do not see wine as an everyday drink. Yet, as FOOD & WINE readers know, wine *should* be a daily pleasure: A glass or two with an evening meal marks a most civilized transition from the working day to the relaxation of evening.

Successfully pairing wine and food really boils down to following two straightforward guidelines. The first and most important factor is your own taste. If you enjoy riesling and want to match it with steak, fine; consider the match successful if you enjoy the result. No bolt from the blue will strike you down.

The other main factor to take into account is body. Some wines have more weight—more substance, more impact—than others. This suggests a direction. If you serve a delicate dish with a brawny wine, that delicacy will be smothered by the weight of the wine. That is where the red-with-meat, white-with-fish "rule" came from. Reds generally have more body than whites and therefore will stand up to rich meats. The rule is logical, yet flexible enough so that you can have endless fun making your own matches.

There are other factors, of course, such as acidity and sweetness, and the pairings in this book illustrate directions to explore as you play the character of a wine off the character of a meal. I have chosen a wide variety of wines and wine styles, to reflect the spirit that informs the menus themselves. These can serve as examples, and then you can begin some serious explorations.

Buy different kinds of whites and reds of varying body from a small wineshop owner who will take the time to steer you to the good choices in your price range. Workaday wines should not be expensive. An index at the back of this book helps you choose a menu to accompany a particular wine you may have or especially like (pages 313-316).

Opening a bottle does not mean you have to drain the bottle. Most wines can stand to be open a day or two, cork reinserted, and are fine for cooking for a few days after that. Half-bottles are another option. As to glassware—don't worry. Everyday wines taste just fine from everyday glasses.

—Wayne Young

Spring

Rotini with Bacon, Sweet Peppers, and Peas (p. 31) and Bitter Greens with Toasted Walnuts (p. 32)

Roast Pork with Balsamic Onion Marmalade (p. 25) with Endive and Roquefort Salad (p. 26)

PRESTO PASTA

There are three reasons this tuna-and-tomato pasta dish is bound to become a classic in your repertoire. It uses ingredients you are almost certain to have on hand; the sauce is ready in the time it takes to cook the linguine; and it's just plain delicious. If you see baby artichokes at the market, snatch them up for a lovely sautéed side dish; if you cannot find any, prepare a crisp salad instead. The unlikely match of humble rhubarb—the northern latitudes' first fruit of the season—and tropical, sensuous mango makes a tempting crumble.

Red works best with this meal of meaty tuna and hearty flavors. An excellent Valpolicella (Secco-Bertani is good—avoid the "big" names) or a Chianti Classico will balance the meal with flavor and medium body.

LINGUINE WITH TOMATO, TUNA, AND FENNEL
Use tuna packed in olive oil for this recipe; look for a good brand from Italy or Spain. If you make this pasta in the summer when tomatoes are at their peak, you can use one and a half pounds, peeled, seeded, and chopped, in place of the canned ones called for here.

½ pound thin linguine
¼ cup olive oil
2 teaspoons minced garlic
½ teaspoon dried red-pepper flakes
½ teaspoon fennel seeds
1 5-ounce can imported tuna packed in olive oil, drained
½ teaspoon coarse salt
1 cup canned crushed tomatoes

½ teaspoon minced lemon zest
2 tablespoons chopped flat-leaf parsley

1. In a large pot of boiling, salted water, cook the linguine until almost done, about 12 minutes. Drain, reserving some of the pasta-cooking water.

2. Meanwhile, in a large stainless-steel frying pan, heat the oil. Add the garlic, red-pepper flakes, and fennel seeds and cook over moderate heat, stirring, until the garlic is just golden. Add the tuna and salt, raise the heat to high, and cook until the tuna begins to sizzle, being careful not to break it up too much. Add the tomatoes with their juices and bring to a boil, then simmer over moderate heat until softened, about 4 minutes. Stir in the lemon zest.

3. Add the linguine to the sauce and cook over moderately low heat for 1 minute. If the pasta seems too dry, add a little of the reserved pasta-cooking water, one tablespoon at a time. Top with the parsley, and serve immediately.

—JOHANNE KILLEEN AND GEORGE GERMON

SAUTÉED BABY ARTICHOKES
These artichokes are little, but they are completely mature vegetables.

GAME PLAN

Heat the oven.

Bake the crumble.

Put one pot of water on to boil for the pasta, another for the artichokes.

Cook the artichokes.

Cook the linguine.

Prepare the tomato tuna sauce and sauté the baby artichokes.

4 tablespoons lemon juice (from about 1 lemon)
8 smallest baby artichokes
2 teaspoons butter
1 tablespoon olive oil
1 small clove garlic, cut into thin slices
Salt and fresh-ground black pepper

1. Bring a medium saucepan of water to a boil. Add 3 tablespoons of the lemon juice to a large glass or stainless-steel bowl filled with water. Working with one artichoke at a time, pull off the dark outer leaves and trim ½ inch off the top. Halve each of the artichokes, and then drop them into the lemon water.

2. Drain the artichokes and cook them in the boiling water until tender when pierced with a knife, about 3 minutes. Drain.

3. Meanwhile, in a large stainless-steel frying pan, melt 1 teaspoon of the butter with the oil. Add the garlic and cook over high heat for 10 seconds. Add the artichokes, season with salt and pepper, and cook, turning once, until golden brown, about 5 minutes. Stir in the remaining 1 tablespoon lemon juice and 1 teaspoon butter.

—GRACE PARISI

RHUBARB MANGO CRUMBLE

You cannot tell a ripe mango by its color. To judge whether it is ready to eat, press lightly; it should give a little, like a ripe avocado.

1 pound rhubarb stalks, cut into ¾-inch pieces
1 large mango, peeled and cut into ¾-inch cubes
⅓ cup plus 2 tablespoons sugar
⅔ cup flour
3 tablespoons yellow cornmeal
½ teaspoon ground ginger
⅛ teaspoon fresh-ground white pepper
Pinch salt
5 tablespoons unsalted butter, cut into ½-inch pieces

1. Heat the oven to 425°. Generously butter a large baking dish. Add the rhubarb and mango, and then add the ⅓ cup of sugar and toss gently to combine.

2. In a food processor, combine the remaining 2 tablespoons sugar with the flour, cornmeal, ginger, pepper, and salt; pulse a few times to mix. Add the butter and process just until the mixture begins to clump. Transfer the topping to a bowl.

3. Pinch the topping to form large and small crumbs and sprinkle them evenly over the fruit. Bake for 25 to 30 minutes, or until bubbly and golden on top. If desired, set the baking dish under the broiler for a few seconds to brown the top.

—GRACE PARISI

SOUTHERN UN-FRIED CHICKEN

Making fried chicken is usually reserved for those days when you are feeling ambitious. For weekdays, our easy un-fried chicken provides a lot of eating satisfaction with much less bother. The skin is removed and a new, crisp coating, made with peppery bread crumbs and flour, forms in the oven. Simple buttermilk biscuits and a hearty salad garnished with pecans contribute to this southern-in-spirit supper.

For dessert, here's something to remind you that summer is not all that far away. Pull out two tall glasses and fix root beer floats with your favorite microbrewed root beer and two scoops of vanilla ice cream.

Southern cooking calls for southern wine—southern Italian, that is. Try Lacryma Christi, a fuller white with some nutty nuances (Mastroberardino is your best bet). If this is unavailable, pick up a bottle of an Australian sémillon/chardonnay blend.

UN-FRIED CHICKEN

This frying-pan-to-oven technique works very well with skin-on pieces of chicken, too.

 1 chicken (about 2½ pounds), cut into 8 pieces, wings and backs reserved for another use
½ cup unseasoned dry bread crumbs
¼ cup flour
 2 teaspoons fresh-ground black pepper
½ teaspoon salt
 2 tablespoons cooking oil

1. Heat the oven to 400°. Using your hands, a knife, and a paper

17

towel (to facilitate your grip), skin the chicken pieces.

2. In a paper or plastic bag, combine the bread crumbs, flour, pepper, and salt and shake to mix. Rinse the chicken in cold water. Pat dry. Place several pieces in the bag and shake until well coated; set aside. Repeat with the remaining chicken.

3. In a shallow, 2-quart casserole or large heavy ovenproof frying pan, heat the oil over moderately high heat. Add all the chicken pieces, skinned-side down, and cook until beginning to brown, 1 to 2 minutes. Place the casserole on the bottom rack of the oven and bake for about 15 minutes, until the chicken is golden brown on the bottom.

4. Remove the casserole from the oven and turn the chicken pieces over with tongs. Return the casserole to the oven and cook for about 20 minutes longer, until the breasts are no longer pink at the bone. Transfer the breasts to a platter. Cook the thighs and legs for 5 more minutes. Transfer to the platter. Serve immediately. Cover and refrigerate leftovers.

—SUSAN SHAPIRO JASLOVE

SPINACH-AND-CABBAGE SALAD WITH PECANS

GAME PLAN

Heat the oven.

Coat and bake the chicken.

Wash the spinach and shred the cabbage; mix the dressing.

Mix the biscuits; bake them on the upper rack of the oven while the chicken cooks.

Toss the salad.

¼ cup pecan halves, chopped
½ pound spinach, stems removed, leaves washed and torn into bite-size pieces
1½ cups shredded red cabbage
½ small red onion, sliced thin
1 tablespoon wine vinegar
¼ teaspoon grainy mustard
2 tablespoons olive oil
2 tablespoons buttermilk
Salt and fresh-ground black pepper

1. Heat the oven to 400°. Spread the pecans in a baking pan and toast, stirring once, for about 8 minutes. Set aside to cool.

2. In a large bowl, toss together the spinach, cabbage, and onion. Refrigerate.

3. In a small glass or stainless-steel bowl, whisk the vinegar with the mustard. Whisk in the oil and then the buttermilk. Season to taste with salt and pepper.

4. Just before serving, toss the salad with the pecans and dressing.

—SUSAN SHAPIRO JASLOVE

BUTTERMILK BISCUITS

Look for whole wheat pastry flour at health-food stores. If you cannot find it, substitute one-quarter cup cake flour and one-quarter cup regular whole wheat flour.

- 1 cup all-purpose flour
- ½ cup whole wheat pastry flour
- 1½ teaspoons baking powder
- ¾ teaspoon salt
- ½ teaspoon baking soda
- ½ teaspoon sugar
- 6 tablespoons cold unsalted butter, cut into small pieces
- ½ cup buttermilk

1. Heat the oven to 400°. In a large bowl, whisk together the flours, baking powder, salt, baking soda, and sugar. Using your fingers or a pastry blender, cut in the butter until the mixture resembles coarse crumbs. Stir in the buttermilk with a fork.

2. Turn the dough out onto a lightly floured surface and knead about 8 times until it just becomes a smooth mass. Pat the dough into an 8-by-4-inch rectangle. Cut the dough into eight 2-inch square biscuits.

3. Place the biscuits about 1 inch apart on an ungreased baking sheet. Bake for about 15 minutes, until golden brown. Serve warm.

—SUSAN SHAPIRO JASLOVE

JAPANESE-STYLE SALMON

This fast dinner, like almost all Japanese fare, features clear, uncomplicated flavors. For a change of pace, you can present the meal as it would be served in the East by emphasizing the individuality of each dish. Begin with the elegant sesame-enhanced spinach, served in a small bowl. Follow with the main course of meaty broiled salmon steaks marinated in a mixture of sake and ginger juice. Crisp stir-fried snow peas and bean sprouts sprinkled with soy sauce and rice-wine vinegar may accompany the salmon on the plate. In Japan, short- or medium-grain sushi-style white rice is usually served in a separate bowl, although it can be put on the plate with the salmon and vegetables.

Oranges are a traditional refreshing end to an Asian meal. Use mandarin oranges if you want to be authentic, or take some culinary license and finish with navel oranges.

Riesling goes with salmon, and this is no exception. The steeliness and peachy fruit of Alsace riesling keep the palate clear to enjoy each bite of flavorful fish. Pinot grigio would make a fine substitute if riesling is not your style.

SPINACH WITH TOASTED SESAME SEEDS
The spinach leaves are blanched for this light first course, which is served at room temperature.

  1 teaspoon sesame seeds
½ pound fresh spinach, stems removed and leaves washed
½ teaspoon lemon juice
¼ teaspoon soy sauce
    Pinch sugar

Pinch salt

1 teaspoon Asian sesame oil

1. Bring a medium saucepan of lightly salted water to a boil. In a small heavy frying pan, toast the sesame seeds over moderate heat, shaking the pan occasionally, until fragrant, about 4 minutes.

2. Add the spinach to the boiling water and cook for 1 minute. Drain, rinse with cold water, and drain again thoroughly; squeeze the spinach dry. Coarsely chop the spinach and transfer to a medium glass or stainless-steel bowl.

3. In a small glass or stainless-steel bowl, combine the lemon juice, soy sauce, sugar, and salt. Stir in the sesame oil. Pour the sesame dressing over the spinach and toss to coat. Let stand at room temperature until ready to serve.

4. Divide the spinach and its dressing between two small bowls or plates, sprinkle with the toasted sesame seeds, and serve.

—KENNETH WAPNER

GINGER-GLAZED SALMON STEAKS
The mild bite of ginger and soy offsets the richness of the fish.

2 tablespoons grated fresh ginger
3 tablespoons sake or dry sherry
2 teaspoons soy sauce
1 teaspoon cooking oil
1 teaspoon dry mustard
  Salt and fresh-ground black pepper
2 salmon steaks, about 1 inch thick (about 6 ounces each)
  Steamed rice for, serving

1. Put the grated ginger in a fine strainer set over a small bowl. Press down on the ginger with the back of a spoon to extract as much juice as possible. Discard the pulp. Stir the sake, soy sauce, oil, and mustard into the ginger juice and season with salt and pepper.

2. Set the salmon steaks in a broiler pan. Pour the ginger marinade over the salmon and turn to coat. Cover and let stand at

GAME PLAN

Marinate the salmon.

Cook the rice.

Cook the spinach, toss it with the sesame dressing, and let stand until serving.

Heat the broiler.

Wash and prepare the vegetables for stir-frying.

Broil the salmon.

Stir-fry the vegetables.

room temperature for 30 to 40 minutes, turning once more.

3. Heat the broiler. Broil the salmon for about 6 minutes, without turning, until the steaks are just cooked through. Transfer the salmon to individual plates. Spoon the pan juices over the salmon and serve with steamed rice.

—Kenneth Wapner

STIR-FRIED SNOW PEAS AND BEAN SPROUTS
Two quick-cooking vegetables provide a slightly crunchy counterpoint to the fish and rice.

1 tablespoon cooking oil
2 ounces bean sprouts (about 1 cup)
4 ounces snow peas, strings removed
2 scallions, including green tops, sliced thin
½ teaspoon rice-wine vinegar
  Soy sauce
  Salt and fresh-ground black pepper

Heat the oil in a wok or large stainless-steel frying pan over high heat until almost smoking. Add the bean sprouts, snow peas, and scallions and stir-fry over moderately high heat until just tender, about 3 minutes. Sprinkle in the vinegar. Season with soy sauce, salt, and pepper and toss. Serve at once.

—Kenneth Wapner

FRENCH TWIST

Here is a three-course meal that is nevertheless quickly and easily made. Ideal for those days that speed by, giving you much to discuss over dinner, it begins with clams cooked in the French style—in a pot with a splash of wine, plenty of garlic, a little butter, and a sprinkling of fresh parsley. For the main course, there is a no-fuss pork tenderloin accompanied by a lively onion marmalade. The sweetness of the marmalade is balanced by the slight bitterness of the endive salad. For dessert, a bittersweet chocolate sorbet, perhaps, and some of your favorite little French butter cookies.

Here's a *real* twist. Drink a California wine made from an Italian variety—like Mondavi's sangiovese—to span international horizons for this meal. A sangiovese-based Tuscan wine like Rosso di Montalcino makes a good alternative.

CLAMS À LA MARINIÈRE
Serve the hot clams in deep bowls with plenty of crusty French bread to sop up the garlicky juices.

- ¼ cup chicken stock or canned low-sodium chicken broth
- ¼ cup plus 2 tablespoons dry white wine
- 1 tablespoon minced garlic
- 1 tablespoon olive oil
- 1½ teaspoons butter
- 1½ dozen littleneck clams, as small as possible, well scrubbed
- 1 tablespoon minced flat-leaf parsley
- Fresh-ground black pepper

In a large stainless-steel saucepan, combine the stock, wine, garlic, oil, and butter; bring to a boil. Add the clams, cover, and cook over high heat until they open, 5 to 8 minutes; remove them as they open. (Discard any that do not open.) Stir the parsley and a generous pinch of pepper into the liquid and pour over the clams.

—Jocelyn Bulow

ROAST PORK WITH BALSAMIC ONION MARMALADE

If you have good strong veal stock in your freezer, skip Step 2 and add a half cup of the veal stock in place of the reduced chicken broth in Step 4.

  1 small onion, cut into thin slices
  3 tablespoons balsamic vinegar
  1 tablespoon sherry vinegar
  1 tablespoon sugar
     Cracked black pepper
  1 cup chicken stock or canned low-sodium chicken broth
  2 tablespoons butter
1½ teaspoons olive oil
  1 pork tenderloin, about ¾ pound, trimmed
     Salt

1. In a small stainless-steel saucepan, combine the onion, balsamic and sherry vinegars, sugar, and ¼ teaspoon of cracked black pepper and bring to a boil over high heat. Reduce the heat to moderately low and cook, stirring occasionally, until the liquid is reduced to a thick syrup and the onion is soft, about 20 minutes. The marmalade can be served chilled or at room temperature. (*The marmalade can be refrigerated in a glass jar for several days.*)

2. Meanwhile, heat the oven to 425°. In a medium saucepan, cook the stock over high heat until reduced to ½ cup, 8 to 10 minutes.

3. In a large ovenproof frying pan, melt 1 tablespoon of the butter with the oil over moderately high heat. When the foam subsides, season the pork lightly with cracked black pepper and cook until browned on all sides, about 2 minutes per side. Transfer the pan to the oven and roast the meat for 8 to 9 minutes, or until an instant-read thermometer inserted in the thickest part

GAME PLAN

Prepare the onion marmalade.

Scrub the clams.

Make the salad.

Heat the oven.

Cook the clams.

Roast the pork while you are enjoying the first course.

25

registers 135°. Transfer the pork to a cutting board and let rest while you finish the sauce.

4. Meanwhile, discard the fat in the frying pan and put the pan over high heat. Add the reduced broth and boil, scraping up any brown bits from the bottom of the pan, until reduced to ¼ cup, about 4 minutes. Remove from the heat and whisk in the remaining 1 tablespoon of butter. Season with salt.

5. Slice the tenderloin across the grain and arrange on two plates. Spoon some of the onion marmalade next to the pork, drizzle the pork with the pan sauce and serve.

—JOCELYN BULOW

ENDIVE-AND-ROQUEFORT SALAD

For a wonderful flavor, toast the walnuts in a dry heavy frying pan over moderate heat for a minute or two before adding to the salad.

  1 tablespoon balsamic vinegar
  2 tablespoons olive oil
  1 tablespoon walnut oil
1½ teaspoons minced fresh chives
     Salt and fresh-ground black pepper
  2 heads Belgian endive, cored and cut crosswise
     into 1-inch pieces
  1 ounce Roquefort, crumbled (about ⅓ cup)
  2 tablespoons chopped walnuts

Pour the vinegar into a glass or stainless-steel bowl. Whisk in the olive oil in a thin stream, and then whisk in the walnut oil. Stir in the chives. Season with salt and pepper, add the endive, and toss. Top with the Roquefort and walnuts and serve.

—JOCELYN BULOW

VEAL WITH LEMON PASTA

When you want a weeknight meal that is elegant and easy, it is worth indulging in boneless veal loin. The cut is lean, tender, and delicious and needs only its meaty pan juices as a sauce. When asparagus is in season, it's hard to get enough. And you will undoubtedly find yourself returning to this almond garlic topping again and again. Orecchiette—the funny little ear-shaped pasta that holds sauces so well—completes the main-course trio. For dessert, splurge on your favorite raspberry sorbet, one that contains only fruit and sugar.

Veal works equally well with an appropriate red *or* white. For a red, try a barbera or a pinot noir. A white with substance, such as a Pouilly-Fuissé or a more costly Condrieu, will complement the pan-roasted flavors admirably.

PAN-ROASTED VEAL STEAKS
If you cannot find veal loin steaks, veal chops work well in this recipe.

2 6-ounce boneless veal loin steaks, about 1¼ inches thick
1 teaspoon olive oil
   Large pinch herbes de Provence or dried thyme
   Salt and fresh-ground black pepper
⅓ cup water

1. Heat the oven to 375°.

2. Rub the veal with the oil and sprinkle with the herbes de Provence and salt and pepper to taste. Heat an ovenproof frying pan over moderately high heat. Add the seasoned veal to the pan and cook, turning once, until well browned, about 1½ minutes per

side. Transfer the pan to the oven and roast until done to your taste, about 8 minutes for medium. Transfer the meat to a plate and keep warm.

3. Add the water to the frying pan and bring to a boil over moderate heat, scraping up any brown bits. Add any accumulated juices from the veal and boil until slightly reduced, about 1 minute.

4. Just before serving, transfer the veal to individual plates and spoon the pan sauce on top.

—TRACEY SEAMAN

ASPARAGUS WITH TOASTED ALMONDS AND GARLIC
Look for tight tips when buying asparagus; they are a sign of freshness.

½ pound pencil-thin asparagus
1 tablespoon olive oil
2 tablespoons slivered almonds
1 clove garlic, sliced thin
   Salt and fresh-ground black pepper
1 tablespoon sherry vinegar
1 teaspoon butter

1. Snap the tough ends off the asparagus and discard them. Bring 1 inch of water to a boil in a large stainless-steel frying pan. Add the asparagus and cook until just tender and bright green, about 3 minutes. Drain and pat dry.

2. Wipe out the frying pan and set it over high heat. Add the oil and heat. Add the almonds and cook, stirring, for 30 seconds. Add the asparagus and garlic, and season with salt and pepper. Cook, stirring frequently, until the garlic and almonds are golden and the asparagus is just beginning to brown, about 4 minutes. Stir in the vinegar and butter, and season with salt and pepper.

—GRACE PARISI

GAME PLAN

Put a pot of water on to boil for the pasta.

Cook the pasta while you make the lemon cream sauce.

Cook the asparagus.

Season the meat, sear it, and then transfer it to the oven to bake.

ORECCHIETTE WITH LEMON PARMESAN CREAM

This pasta dish is also a wonderful accompaniment to salmon or shrimp.

- 4 ounces orecchiette or farfalle
- 1 tablespoon butter
- 1 tablespoon lemon juice
- ⅓ cup heavy cream
- ¼ cup grated Parmesan
- 2 tablespoons minced fresh chives
- 1 teaspoon grated lemon zest (from 1 lemon)
  Salt and fresh-ground black pepper

1. In a large saucepan of boiling, salted water, cook the orecchiette, stirring frequently, until just done, about 11 minutes. Drain and return the pasta to the pan.

2. Meanwhile, in a small stainless-steel saucepan, melt the butter with the lemon juice and cream over moderately low heat. Reduce the heat to low and cook until the cream is barely simmering, about 5 minutes.

3. Just before serving, stir the cream sauce into the pasta. Add the Parmesan, chives, and lemon zest, season with salt and pepper, and toss.

—TRACEY SEAMAN

Pasta, Peppers, and Peas

In this superfast pasta recipe, bacon infuses rotini with a smoky warmth. Bell peppers and peas add color and texture. Bitter greens tossed with walnuts and Roquefort cheese provide a salad and a cheese course in one. The choice of greens is yours; watercress, arugula, Belgian endive, chicory, escarole, or radicchio will not be overwhelmed by the assertive cheese and the toasted nuts. The meal ends with a simple but splendid dessert of fresh sliced pineapple with piña colada flavorings.

An earthy, medium-bodied red wine will mesh well with the rustic style of the meal. Try a modern-style Rioja (such as a Martinez-Bujanda) or, for more zippy acidity, go with a Nebbiolo delle Langhe.

ROTINI WITH BACON, SWEET PEPPERS, AND PEAS

If you can find them, English peas are wonderful here, but they must be garden-fresh and not too big. Frozen petite peas are a fine substitute.

¼ pound bacon slices, cut into 1-inch-wide pieces
1 tablespoon olive oil
1 small onion, sliced thin
1 small green bell pepper, cut into long, thin strips
1 small red or yellow bell pepper, cut into long, thin strips,
   or a combination
   Salt
½ cup half-and-half
   Fresh-ground black pepper
½ pound rotini, or other short corkscrew pasta
½ cup fresh or frozen peas

1. In a large frying pan, fry the bacon over moderately high heat, spooning off the fat as it collects in the pan, until all the fat is rendered and the bacon is lightly browned, 5 to 7 minutes. Using a slotted spoon, transfer the bacon to paper towels to drain. Discard the bacon fat from the pan.

2. Add the oil to the pan, and then add the onion, bell peppers, and ¼ teaspoon salt. Cover and cook over moderate heat, stirring frequently, until the vegetables are softened, about 10 minutes. Reduce the heat to low and stir in the bacon. Add the half-and-half and cook until reduced and slightly thickened, about 1 minute. Season to taste with salt and pepper.

3. Meanwhile, in a large pot of boiling, salted water, cook the pasta until just barely tender, about 12 minutes. Add the peas and cook for 2 minutes longer. Drain and toss with the sauce. Serve immediately.

—STEPHANIE LYNESS

BITTER GREENS WITH TOASTED WALNUTS

If you do not have walnut oil, use a fruity extra-virgin olive oil.

GAME PLAN

Slice the pineapple and combine with the piña colada flavorings.

Put a pot of water on to boil for the pasta.

Toast the walnuts in a hot oven.

Prepare the sauce and cook the pasta.

Make the vinaigrette.

Toss the pasta with the sauce and the greens with the vinaigrette.

- ¼ cup walnuts, chopped
- 2 teaspoons sherry vinegar or other wine vinegar
  Salt and fresh-ground black pepper
- 1 tablespoon olive oil
- 1 teaspoon walnut oil
- 4 to 5 cups mixed bitter greens, cut or torn in pieces
- 1 ounce Roquefort, crumbled (about ¼ cup)

1. Heat the oven to 425°. Spread the nuts on a rimmed baking sheet and toast in the oven until fragrant, 7 to 10 minutes.

2. In a small glass or stainless-steel bowl, whisk the vinegar with a pinch each of salt and pepper. Whisk in the olive oil and walnut oil. Toss the greens with the vinaigrette, Roquefort, and walnuts.

—STEPHANIE LYNESS

SALAD GREENS: HOW MUCH TO BUY

Many recipes such as the one on the previous page call for cups of washed and torn salad greens, but how do you know how many cups are in a head of escarole or a bunch of arugula? Here are some rough guidelines.

UNTRIMMED	TRIMMED
1 bunch arugula (6 ounces)	2 cups
1 head escarole (12 ounces)	6 cups
1 head radicchio (8 ounces)	1 cup
1 bunch watercress (5 ounces)	2½ cups

PINEAPPLE COLADA

- 2 cups diced fresh pineapple
- 1 tablespoon lime juice
- 1 tablespoon sugar
- 1 tablespoon shredded sweet coconut
- 1 tablespoon light or dark rum

In a medium bowl, combine the pineapple, lime juice, sugar, coconut, and rum. Stir and let stand at room temperature for 1 hour. Spoon into small bowls and serve.

—STEPHANIE LYNESS

PITA PIZZAS

Pitas make great quick and crusty pizzas, and they are the perfect match for any ingredients you want to arrange on top. In this recipe, prosciutto, onion, and cheese are the toppings along with a simple no-cook sauce made from crushed, drained canned tomatoes. A touch of red-pepper flakes sprinkled on at the end spices things up a bit. Serve a crunchy endive and grated-carrot salad on the side.

Ripe pears, your favorite biscotti, and a small glass of grappa provide a delicious, uncomplicated finish to this hearty dinner. Italians like to serve grappa—a powerful digestive spirit—after a meal. Bosc pears are still sweet, crisp, and refreshing in the spring; buy your them few days ahead to give the fruit time to mellow.

For a meal this simple, keep the wine simple. A fresh Chianti or Montepulciano d'Abruzzo would be the perfect companion for the tart, sweet, and salty flavors of the tomato, onion, and prosciutto on the pizza.

PROSCIUTTO-AND-ONION PITA PIZZAS

The simple technique of starting the pizzas on the bottom rack of a very hot oven and then switching to the top rack for the final few minutes results in an extra-crisp crust.

  1 28-ounce can Italian peeled tomatoes, drained
  4 8-inch pitas
  2 teaspoons olive oil
  1 small red onion, cut into thin slices
  2 ounces thin-sliced prosciutto, cut into 1-inch-wide strips
1½ cups grated mozzarella (¼ pound)

1½ cups grated Monterey jack (¼ pound)
¼ cup grated Parmesan
   Dried red-pepper flakes

1. Pinch the stem ends off the tomatoes and discard. Break the tomatoes into medium-size pieces with your fingers. Put the tomatoes into a colander set over a bowl; shake the colander and set it aside for about 20 minutes to drain as much liquid as possible.

2. Heat the oven to 500°. Place the pitas on a large baking sheet. Brush the outer ridge of each pita with a little of the oil. Spread a quarter of the drained tomatoes on each pita. Sprinkle with a quarter of the onion slices, prosciutto strips, and grated mozzarella and Monterey jack. Sprinkle each pizza with 1 tablespoon of the Parmesan.

3. Bake the pizzas on the bottom rack of the oven for 10 minutes. Move them to the top rack and continue baking for about 4 minutes, or until the cheese starts to brown. Remove from the oven and let the pizzas stand on the baking sheet for 2 to 3 minutes to crisp the bottoms. Sprinkle the pizzas with dried red-pepper flakes to taste and serve immediately.

—MARCIA KIESEL

ENDIVE-AND-CARROT SALAD

The beauty of endive for quick weeknight suppers is that you do not have to wash it repeatedly like many salad greens.

1½ teaspoons yellow mustard seeds
 1 small clove garlic, minced
 1 teaspoon lemon juice
 ½ teaspoon Dijon mustard
1½ tablespoons olive oil
   Salt and fresh-ground black pepper
 4 heads Belgian endive, cored and cut into
   ½-inch-thick slices
 1 small carrot, grated

1. In a small frying pan, toast the mustard seeds over high heat

GAME PLAN

Heat the oven.

Drain the tomatoes.

Grate the carrots for salad, and then the cheese for the pizzas.

Assemble and bake the pizzas.

Slice the endive and assemble the salad.

until fragrant and lightly browned, about 1 minute. Transfer the mustard seeds to a plate and let cool.

2. In a small glass or stainless-steel bowl, mix together the garlic, lemon juice, mustard, and oil. Season with salt and pepper.

3. In a medium glass or stainless-steel bowl, toss the endive with the carrot. Add the dressing and toss well. Sprinkle the salad with the mustard seeds.

—MARCIA KIESEL

ABOUT BELGIAN ENDIVE

Although it is white, not green, Belgian endive is known as a bitter green. The plants are grown in darkness to prevent the leaves from turning green; often you will find heads of Belgian endive wrapped in dark blue paper to prevent any coloring of the leaves during transport. In salads, endive adds a bittersweet crunch. Braised endive is a fine match for full-flavored meats.

CREAMY FETTUCCINE WITH CHICKEN

An all-in-one pasta dish is ideal for a quick weeknight dinner. Here fettuccine is tossed with strips of sautéed chicken and spinach and coated with a creamy sauce studded with chopped tomatoes. Grated Parmesan, tossed in just before serving, melts into the mix. As an accompaniment to the pasta, there are savory oven-roasted green beans. If you want to add another side dish—something really fast and fresh—toss sliced raw fennel with a little lemon juice, olive oil, salt, and pepper.

Roasted bananas make an appealing dessert. Place the fruit, peeled and cut in half lengthwise, in a baking dish, sprinkle it with lemon juice and a touch of sugar, and roast alongside the green beans for ten minutes. Lime is excellent, but any citrus sorbet will complement the bananas.

A fresh, unoaked chardonnay from New Zealand is a great match—flavorful and acidic enough to cut through the creamy sauce. Other big chardonnays with little or no oak would work well, too, such as a St-Aubin.

FETTUCCINE WITH CREAMY CHICKEN AND SPINACH

To make this quick dish even quicker, use ten ounces of thawed, drained frozen spinach in place of the fresh.

  2 tablespoons butter
  2 boneless, skinless chicken breasts (about 4 ounces each),
     cut into 1-by-½-inch strips
  ½ pound fresh spinach, stems removed, leaves washed
     and chopped
     Salt and fresh-ground black pepper

Pinch grated nutmeg
½ cup drained canned Italian peeled tomatoes, chopped
½ cup heavy cream
6 ounces fettuccine
¼ cup grated Parmesan, plus more for serving

1. Melt the butter in a heavy frying pan. Add the chicken strips and sauté over moderately high heat just until lightly browned and cooked through, 1 to 2 minutes. Transfer the chicken to a plate.

2. Add the spinach to the frying pan, season with salt, pepper, and nutmeg, and cook over moderately high heat, stirring occasionally, until wilted, about 2 minutes. Add the tomatoes and cook, stirring, until heated through, about 3 minutes. Stir in the cream in a steady stream and simmer the sauce until slightly thickened, about 3 minutes. Season with salt and pepper.

3. Meanwhile, in a large pot of boiling, salted water, cook the fettuccine until just done, about 8 minutes. Drain and return the fettuccine to the pot.

4. Add the chicken strips to the cream sauce and stir over moderate heat until warmed through. Add the chicken and cream sauce to the fettuccine with the ¼ cup Parmesan and toss to coat. Pass additional Parmesan at the table.

—NANCY VERDE BARR

VARIATIONS
Punch up the dish by using black-pepper fettuccine (available at many supermarkets and specialty-food stores) and a large pinch of dried red-pepper flakes, which can be added to the sauce with the tomatoes. Or add a peppery bite by replacing the spinach with arugula.

GAME PLAN

Heat the oven.

Roast the beans and apricots.

Put water on to boil for pasta.

Cook the chicken and the spinach. Make the sauce.

Slice the fennel and toss with lemon juice and olive oil.

Cook the pasta.

Rewarm the chicken in the sauce while the pasta cooks.

ROASTED GREEN BEANS WITH GARLIC

½ pound green beans, stem ends removed and
   tender tips left on
1 clove garlic, smashed
1 sprig thyme
2 tablespoons olive oil
   Salt and fresh-ground black pepper
1 anchovy fillet, mashed
1 to 2 teaspoons lemon juice
½ teaspoon grated lemon zest

1. Heat the oven to 450°. In a large baking dish, toss the green beans with the smashed garlic, thyme, and oil and season with salt and pepper. Spread the beans and seasonings in a single layer and roast for about 15 minutes, tossing occasionally, until tender and lightly browned. Discard the thyme sprig.

2. Transfer the green beans to a bowl. Add the anchovy, lemon juice, and lemon zest and toss well to coat. Serve the roasted green beans warm or at room temperature.

—NANCY VERDE BARR

SHRIMP AND SCALLOPS ON SKEWERS

The simplicity of this menu demands the freshest of ingredients. Shrimp, scallops, and asparagus are all prepared quite plainly, in order to taste magnificently of themselves. Grilled or broiled seafood skewers are served on a bed of yellow-hued orzo. Although orzo is often used in soups and sometimes in salads, the recipe that follows treats this pasta like rice in a pilaf: The grains made from durum wheat are sautéed in olive oil before being simmered in saffron-flavored water. The result is something like a creamy risotto. Warm asparagus with a very light lemony vinaigrette stands in for a salad. Fresh strawberries make an appropriate finale.

Light seafood takes on heartier flavors after even short contact with a hot grill. This dish will stand up to a good quality Vernaccia di San Gimignano or a lighter style white Burgundy, such as a Mâcon.

GRILLED SHRIMP AND SCALLOPS

Thread the shrimp and scallops onto separate skewers because the cooking times of the two seafoods differ. If you are using bamboo skewers, soak them in water for ten minutes beforehand so they won't burn.

6 ounces large shrimp (8 to 10), shelled and deveined
6 ounces large sea scallops (8 to 10), membrane removed
  Olive oil, for brushing
  Salt and fresh-ground black pepper

1. Light the grill or heat the broiler. Thread 4 to 5 shrimp on each of two 8-inch skewers. Thread 4 to 5 scallops on each of two

more skewers. Brush the seafood with oil and season lightly with salt and pepper.

2. Grill or broil the seafood, turning the skewers once, until just cooked through, about 2 minutes on each side for the shrimp and 3 minutes on each side for the scallops.

—STEPHANIE LYNESS

ORZO WITH SAFFRON

For extra flavor and richness, you can substitute canned chicken broth for the water. Choose a reduced-sodium broth, and cut the amount of salt in the recipe.

    2   teaspoons olive oil
    ¾   cup orzo
    1¼ cups boiling water, more if needed
    1   teaspoon butter
    ¼   teaspoon salt
        Pinch saffron threads
        Fresh-ground black pepper

1. In a medium saucepan, heat the oil over moderate heat. Add the orzo and cook, stirring, until well coated with the oil, 1 to 2 minutes.

2. Stir in the water, butter, salt, and saffron and bring to a boil. Reduce the heat to moderately low, cover, and simmer until the pasta is tender, most of the water has been absorbed, and the mixture is creamy, about 15 minutes. If necessary, stir in additional hot water in small increments and cook a little bit longer, stirring occasionally, to achieve the right consistency. Season to taste with pepper and serve immediately.

—STEPHANIE LYNESS

GAME PLAN

Light the grill or heat the broiler.

Cook the asparagus.

Start the orzo.

Make the lemon vinaigrette.

Grill or broil the seafood skewers.

ASPARAGUS WITH LEMON VINAIGRETTE

If you choose very fresh, pencil-thin asparagus spears, you will not have to peel the stalks before cooking.

¾ pound asparagus
⅛ teaspoon grated lemon zest
2 teaspoons lemon juice
1½ tablespoons olive oil
   Salt and fresh-ground black pepper
2 teaspoons sliced scallion

1. Snap the tough ends off the asparagus and discard them. In a large pot of boiling salted water, cook the asparagus until just tender, about 3 minutes. Drain thoroughly and transfer to a serving plate.

2. In a small glass or stainless-steel bowl, whisk the lemon zest and lemon juice. Gradually whisk in the oil. Season to taste with salt and pepper.

3. Spoon the vinaigrette evenly over the asparagus and sprinkle the scallion on top. Serve warm or at room temperature.

—STEPHANIE LYNESS

CLAMS WITH A SPANISH ACCENT

Just because you are making a Spanish dish with rice and shell-fish does not mean it has to be paella. Unlike that time-consuming old standard, this quick savory main course from the Basque region makes the succulent clams, not the rice, the main feature. A pungent garlic-and-parsley-packed green sauce tops the clams, which are served on a bed of buttery rice pilaf; the sauce is delicious with any seafood. The accompanying asparagus salad has a tart dressing made with roasted peppers, a favorite in-gredient in Spanish cooking.

If you can find an albariño, a Spanish white wine with good acidity and peachy flavors, drink it with this meal to keep up the Iberian theme. If it's unavailable, a vinho verde from Portugal or even a dry New York State riesling would work well.

CLAMS WITH GARLIC SAUCE
Garlic, parsley, and chile brighten this dish of tender clams. Soaking the clams in water with cornmeal helps remove any sand they might contain.

2 dozen littleneck clams, scrubbed
¼ cup cornmeal
1 teaspoon coarse salt
2 cloves garlic, minced
3 tablespoons minced fresh parsley
A few saffron threads
2 tablespoons olive oil
½ small onion, minced
¼ cup dry white wine
2 teaspoons lemon juice

1 small, dried red chile pepper
1 bay leaf
⅛ teaspoon hot paprika
  Fresh-ground black pepper
¼ cup fish stock or 2 tablespoons bottled clam juice
  diluted with 2 tablespoons water

1. In a bowl, cover the clams and cornmeal with water; add the salt. Soak for 45 minutes; drain and rinse.

2. In a blender or mini-processor, puree the garlic with 2 tablespoons of the parsley and the saffron.

3. Heat the oil in a large stainless-steel frying pan. Add the onion and cook over moderate heat until translucent. Add the clams, wine, lemon juice, chile, bay leaf, paprika, and black pepper. Cover, raise the heat to high, and bring to a boil. Cook, shaking the pan occasionally, just until the clams open, about 3 minutes. Remove the open clams. Continue to cook, uncovering the pan as necessary to remove the clams as soon as their shells open.

4. Add the fish stock and the garlic mixture to the pan and cook until the sauce is slightly thickened, about 1 minute. Discard the chile and bay leaf. Put the clams over the rice (recipe below), spoon the garlic sauce on top, and sprinkle with the remaining 1 tablespoon parsley.

—Penelope Casas

BAKED RICE WITH PARSLEY

1 tablespoon butter
2 tablespoons minced onion
½ cup medium-grain rice, such as Valencia or arborio
1¼ cups fish stock or ¾ cup bottled clam juice
  diluted with ½ cup of water
1 tablespoon minced fresh parsley
  Salt

1. Heat the oven to 400°. Melt the butter in a small ovenproof saucepan. Add the onion and cook over high heat, stirring, until

GAME PLAN

Soak the clams. Bring the asparagus water to a boil.

Heat the oven.

Prepare the ingredients for the garlic sauce.

Start the rice.

Cook the asparagus. Make the vinaigrette, dress the asparagus, and let stand at room temperature.

Cook the clams and make the garlic sauce.

translucent, about 2 minutes. Add the rice and stir until the grains are coated. Add the stock, parsley, and a pinch of salt, and bring to a boil. Stir the rice, cover, and bake for 18 minutes. Remove from the oven and let stand, covered, for 10 minutes. Stir the rice and season with more salt.

—PENELOPE CASAS

ASPARAGUS WITH RED-PEPPER VINAIGRETTE

Save the leftover dressing to spoon over steamed broccoli or toss with a crisp green salad. Bottled roasted peppers that are deep red have the best flavor.

  10 ounces asparagus
  ¼ cup olive oil
 1½ tablespoons wine vinegar
   1 tablespoon chopped bottled roasted red pepper (pimiento)
   1 small clove garlic, smashed
  ½ teaspoon minced fresh thyme
  ¼ teaspoon Dijon mustard
      Pinch sugar
      Salt and fresh-ground black pepper

1. Snap the tough ends off the asparagus and discard them. In a frying pan of boiling, salted water, cook the asparagus over high heat until just tender, about 3 minutes. Drain well and transfer to two plates.

2. In a mini-processor, combine the oil, vinegar, red pepper, garlic, thyme, mustard, sugar, salt, and black pepper; blend until smooth. Drizzle half of the dressing over the asparagus and serve.

—PENELOPE CASAS

LEMONGRASS BASS

Braising fish fillets in wine is a quintessentially French technique. Adding aromatic lemongrass, an ingredient ubiquitous in Thai and Vietnamese cuisines, lends an Asian sensibility. But whatever the origins, the flavors meld wonderfully with the mild fish. Sautéed spinach with shiitakes—a mushroom much loved in Japan—contributes to the Asian accent. For a quick, crunchy relish, grate daikon radish and toss it with a little rice-wine vinegar. For dessert, there is an especially gingery gingerbread. The recipe makes enough for six, so you can have a slice with your morning coffee.

Try something a little unusual tonight, such as an Alsace sylvaner. Rationale: Fine fish, such as sea bass, needs a spicy, high-acid wine to enhance its inherent delicacy. For a fancier meal, look for a first-rate Chablis, such as Vincent or Moreau.

SEA BASS WITH WHITE WINE AND LEMONGRASS

If your fishmonger does not have sea bass, this recipe is equally good made with red snapper or grouper.

> 3 teaspoons butter
> 1 shallot, minced
> 1 stalk lemongrass, bottom third only, pounded flat and chopped fine, or ¼ teaspoon grated lemon zest
> 2 sea-bass fillets with skin (about 6 ounces each)
>   Salt and fresh-ground black pepper
> ¼ cup dry white wine
> ¼ cup water
> 1 tablespoon minced fresh parsley

1. Heat the oven to 425°. Rub 1 teaspoon of the butter over the bottom of an ovenproof frying pan just large enough to hold the fish fillets. Sprinkle the shallot and lemongrass on top. Slash the skin of each fillet in 2 or 3 places. Season the fillets with salt and pepper and place skin-side down in the pan. Pour the wine and water around the fillets and bring to a simmer over moderately low heat. Cover the pan, transfer to the oven, and bake for 8 to 9 minutes, until the fish is just cooked through.

2. Transfer the fillets to plates and keep warm. Place the frying pan over moderately high heat and boil the sauce until reduced by half, adding any liquid from the fish plates. Remove from the heat and whisk in the remaining 2 teaspoons butter and the parsley. Season with salt and pepper and spoon the sauce over the fish.

—STEPHANIE LYNESS

SAUTÉED SPINACH WITH SHIITAKE MUSHROOMS

½ teaspoon sesame seeds
2 teaspoons cooking oil
4 ounces shiitake mushrooms, stems removed and
   caps cut into thin slices
   Salt
1 pound spinach, stems removed and leaves washed
   Fresh-ground black pepper

1. In a small frying pan, toast the sesame seeds over moderate heat, stirring, until fragrant, about 5 minutes.

2. In a large stainless-steel frying pan, heat the oil over moderately high heat. Add the mushrooms, season with salt, and cook until softened, about 5 minutes. Transfer to a plate.

3. Wipe out the large frying pan. Add the spinach with the water clinging to it, season with salt and pepper, and cook, stirring, until all the water has evaporated, about 7 minutes. Stir in the mushrooms. Serve sprinkled with the toasted sesame seeds.

—STEPHANIE LYNESS

GAME PLAN

Heat the oven.

Mix and bake the gingerbread.

Cook the rice.

Bake the fish.

Prepare the vegetable accompaniments.

RICH GINGERBREAD

This moist cake will sink slightly after it comes out of the oven.

  2 cups flour
  1 teaspoon baking soda
  ¾ teaspoon salt
1½ teaspoons ground ginger
  1 teaspoon cinnamon
  ½ teaspoon ground allspice
12 tablespoons unsalted butter, at room temperature
  ½ cup light brown sugar
  1 egg
  ¾ cup molasses
  ¾ cup milk
     Unsweetened whipped cream

1. Heat the oven to 350°. Butter a 9-inch round cake pan. In a bowl, sift the flour with the baking soda, salt, ginger, cinnamon, and allspice. In a large bowl, cream the butter and brown sugar. Beat in the egg and then the molasses. Add the dry ingredients and the milk in 5 parts, beginning and ending with the dry ingredients and beating after each addition just to mix.

2. Using a rubber spatula, scrape the batter into the prepared pan and smooth the top. Bake for about 50 minutes, until a tester inserted in the center of the cake comes out clean and the side pulls away slightly from the pan. Transfer to a wire rack to cool for 15 minutes. Cut into wedges and serve with the whipped cream. (*The gingerbread will keep for up to 1 week; wrap well and refrigerate.*)

—STEPHANIE LYNESS

GINGER-GLAZED CHICKEN

L ike most good things, the ideas behind this menu are simple
and straightforward. Concoct a glaze of four basic ingredients—fresh ginger, garlic, oil, and teriyaki sauce—then
briefly marinate the chicken in it before baking. The spicy-sweet
marinade transforms ordinary chicken into something special. As
the bird roasts, its fat mellows the hot edge of the ginger while the
sugar in the teriyaki sauce browns and crisps the skin.

Serve this tasty chicken with steamed sugar snap peas; when at
their peak, these tender pods need no embellishment. A warm
salad of watercress and couscous requires only boiling water, a bit
of chopping and a squeeze of lemon. And for dessert, top a luxuri-
ous strawberry mousse with garden-fresh mint.

A California Fumé Blanc, combining ripe fruit and a little
oak with sauvignon blanc's liveliness, will complement all
the flavors here. An alternative approach for bargain hunters: a
southern French chardonnay with just a little oak, such as Fortant
de France.

GINGER-GLAZED CHICKEN

*The sweet, pungent glaze is as good on bone-in chicken breasts as it is on
legs. Or, if you are a fan of chicken wings, use them in place of the legs.*

2 to 2½ ounces fresh ginger (a piece about 3 inches long)
   1 clove garlic, peeled
   1 tablespoon cooking oil
2½ tablespoons teriyaki sauce
   2 whole chicken legs (about 1¾ pounds), halved at the joint
     Salt and fresh-ground black pepper

1. Heat the oven to 450°. Using the side of a teaspoon, scrape the skin from the ginger. Cut the ginger into 1-inch pieces. Put the ginger, garlic, and oil in a food processor or blender and process until the ginger and garlic are chopped fine. With the machine on, add the teriyaki sauce and process until the mixture is the texture of mustard.

2. In a shallow bowl, slather the ginger glaze over the chicken and let marinate for 10 minutes at room temperature.

3. Set the chicken pieces on a broiler pan skin-side up, season with salt and pepper, and bake for about 20 minutes, turning once, until cooked through. Turn the chicken skin-side up and broil for about 1 minute to crisp the skin.

—STEPHANIE LYNESS

COUSCOUS WITH LEMON AND WATERCRESS

1 cup water
2 teaspoons butter
  Salt
⅔ cup couscous
1 bunch watercress, stems removed, leafy parts cut
  crosswise into ½-inch pieces
1 medium scallion, including green top, sliced thin
1 clove garlic, crushed through a press
3 tablespoons lemon juice
1 tablespoon olive oil
1 tablespoon chopped flat-leaf parsley
  Fresh-ground black pepper

1. In a medium saucepan, combine the water with the butter and ¼ teaspoon salt and bring to a boil. Stir in the couscous. Cover. Remove the pan from the heat and let the couscous stand for 5 minutes.

2. Fluff the couscous with a fork. Stir in the watercress, cover and let stand until wilted, about 15 minutes. Stir in the scallion, garlic, lemon juice, oil, and parsley. Season with salt and pepper. Serve the couscous at room temperature.

—STEPHANIE LYNESS

GAME PLAN

Heat the oven.

Prepare the glaze and marinate the chicken.

Bake the chicken.

Prepare the strawberries.

Cook the couscous.

Whip the cream and make the mousse.

Steam the sugar snap peas.

STRAWBERRY MINT MOUSSE

>   1   cup strawberries, hulled and quartered
>   1½   tablespoons sugar
>   ¼   cup sour cream
>   ¼   cup heavy cream
>   Slivered fresh mint, for garnish

1. In a medium bowl, sprinkle the strawberries with the sugar and mash lightly with a fork until the strawberries have exuded some juice and the sugar begins to dissolve. Let stand for 15 minutes.

2. Strain the juice from the strawberries into another bowl. Whisk the sour cream into the juice. In a medium bowl, whip the heavy cream to soft peaks. Fold in the sour cream mixture. Gently fold in the strawberries. Refrigerate until chilled, at least 20 minutes. Spoon the mousse into bowls and garnish with the mint.

—STEPHANIE LYNESS

GREEK BAKED SHRIMP

Greek food is characterized by its bright, intense flavors—briny seafood, tangy lemon, an abundance of herbs, particularly dill. This baked shrimp dish is usually prepared with a thickened tomato sauce; the light egg custard used here makes the dish more elegant. Cucumber-and-bell-pepper salad, dressed with lemon (of course), and buttered orzo are simple, welcoming side dishes. Honey-drenched baklava from a pastry shop or Greek specialty store rounds out the meal nicely.

A racy sauvignon blanc from New Zealand or France's Loire Valley makes a perfect pairing with feta cheese. Avoid oaky sauvignon blancs from California, which would overwhelm the delicacy of the shrimp.

SHRIMP-AND-FETA CASSEROLES WITH DILL
Let the casseroles stand for five minutes before serving.

- 1½ teaspoons olive oil
- 2 large scallions, including green tops, minced
- 1 small clove garlic, minced
- ½ pound medium shrimp, shelled
- 2 plum tomatoes, seeded and diced
- 2 ounces feta, crumbled (about ¼ cup)
- 1 large egg, lightly beaten
- 1½ teaspoons minced fresh dill, or ½ teaspoon dried dill
  Dash hot-pepper sauce
  Salt and fresh-ground black pepper
- ¼ cup heavy cream
- 1 tablespoon grated Parmesan

1. Heat the oven to 400°. Butter two gratin or shallow baking dishes, about 5 inches in diameter.

2. Heat the oil in a small frying pan. Add the scallions and cook over moderately high heat, stirring frequently, until softened, about 2 minutes Add the garlic and cook, stirring, for 1 minute longer. Spread the mixture in the prepared baking dishes and arrange the shrimp on top. Sprinkle with the tomatoes and feta.

3. In a bowl, beat the egg with the dill, hot-pepper sauce, salt, and black pepper. Beat in the cream. Spoon the custard over the shrimp. Sprinkle with the Parmesan. Bake for about 12 minutes, until the custard is set and the shrimp are cooked through.

—BOB CHAMBERS

LEMONY CUCUMBER SALAD

This salad is quite pretty when you use a mixture of bell peppers.

  1 unpeeled English cucumber, halved lengthwise and
      cut into ¼-inch-thick slices
  1 medium red or yellow bell pepper, or a mixture,
      cut into 1-by-¼-inch matchsticks
      Salt
1½ tablespoons lemon juice
 ½ teaspoon Dijon mustard
2½ tablespoons olive oil
  1 tablespoon minced fresh chives
      Fresh-ground black pepper

1. In a colander, toss the cucumbers and bell pepper with ½ teaspoon salt. Let stand at room temperature for 30 minutes to drain.

2. In a glass or stainless-steel bowl, whisk the lemon juice with the mustard. Whisk in the oil and chives; season with salt and black pepper.

3. Transfer the cucumbers and bell peppers to a medium glass or stainless-steel bowl. Add the lemon dressing and toss to combine.

—BOB CHAMBERS

GAME PLAN

Heat the oven.

Put water on to boil for orzo.

Salt the cucumbers and bell peppers.

Assemble and bake the shrimp casserole.

Cook the orzo. Toss the cucumber salad.

PASTA GRATINÉE

This simple taste-of-Italy meatless meal consists of a hearty combination of gratinéed pasta and a garlicky green vegetable, capped off with an instant ice cream dessert. For the main dish, ziti is tossed with a quickly cooked tomato sauce, fresh spinach, and cheese, then run under the broiler to make it golden brown. The broccoli accompaniment is garnished with flavorful, crisp bits of garlic. Vanilla ice cream drizzled with amaretto and sprinkled with amaretti-cookie crumbs completes this satisfying dinner.

Try something fruity and light with this pasta. A northern Italian merlot is now a relatively easy find, or you might experiment with an international combination—Italian pasta and the bright fruity flavors of French Beaujolais.

GRATINÉED ZITI AND SPINACH

Featuring familiar flavors and readily available ingredients, this appealing gratin can be doubled easily if friends should appear.

- 1 tablespoon olive oil
- 1 small onion, diced
- 1 large clove garlic, minced
- 1½ cups canned Italian peeled tomatoes with their juice (one 14-ounce can)
  Pinch dried red-pepper flakes
  Salt and fresh-ground black pepper
- 6 ounces ziti
- ½ pound spinach, stems removed, leaves washed and chopped
- 3 ounces part-skim mozzarella, diced (about ½ cup)
- 8 tablespoons grated Parmesan

1. In a medium stainless-steel frying pan, heat the oil over moderate heat. Add the onion and garlic and cook, stirring occasionally, until the onion is softened, about 5 minutes. Using your hands, break up the tomatoes and add them with their juice to the frying pan. Stir in the red-pepper flakes. Increase the heat to moderately high and boil the sauce, stirring, until most of the liquid has evaporated, about 15 minutes. Season with salt and black pepper. Keep warm.

2. Meanwhile, heat the broiler. Cook the ziti in a large saucepan of boiling, salted water until just done, 9 to 11 minutes. Drain well and return to the dry pan. Stir in the spinach, mozzarella, and 3 tablespoons of the Parmesan. Add the tomato sauce and toss.

3. Transfer the hot ziti to a shallow 10-inch oval gratin dish and sprinkle the remaining 5 tablespoons Parmesan on top. Broil for 1 to 2 minutes, until browned. Serve at once.

—SUSAN SHAPIRO JASLOVE

BROCCOLI WITH GARLIC CHIPS

For garlic fanatics, increase the garlic to taste.

¾ pound broccoli (about 1 stalk)
1 cup water
2 tablespoons olive oil
3 cloves garlic, cut lengthwise into thin slices
  Salt and fresh-ground black pepper

1. Using a small sharp knife, peel off the outer woody layer of the broccoli stalks and trim 1 to 2 inches from the bottom. Cut each broccoli stalk lengthwise to make long "trees," about ½ inch thick each.

2. In a frying pan, bring the water to a boil over high heat. Add the broccoli and cook uncovered, turning the stalks once, until they are tender and the water evaporates, 5 to 6 minutes. Transfer the broccoli to a bowl and set aside.

3. Wipe out the frying pan. Add the oil and heat over moderate heat until hot. Add the garlic and cook, stirring frequently, until

GAME PLAN

Make the tomato sauce for the ziti.

Heat the oven.

Put a pot of water on to boil for the pasta.

Cook the broccoli and the ziti.

just golden brown, about 3 minutes; do not burn the garlic. Using a slotted spoon, transfer the garlic to a paper towel to drain.

4. Add the broccoli to the oil in the frying pan and cook over moderately high heat until heated through, browned in spots, and tender, about 3 minutes. Season to taste with salt and pepper. Arrange on a serving platter with the garlic chips scattered over the top.

—SUSAN SHAPIRO JASLOVE

VANILLA ICE CREAM WITH AMARETTO

Amaretti di Saronno are the best known of these meringue cookies, and the most expensive. Look for alternative brands in Italian specialty shops and cafés.

Vanilla ice cream
About 4 teaspoons amaretto
2 imported Italian amaretti cookies, finely crumbled

Scoop the ice cream into two sundae dishes or glass bowls. Drizzle about 2 generous teaspoons of the amaretto over each serving and sprinkle the amaretti on top. Serve at once.

—SUSAN SHAPIRO JASLOVE

REASON TO CELEBRATE

F ilet mignon is the perfect choice for a cozy celebration of one of life's little occasions—a promotion, a birthday, or maybe just the fact that it's Friday night. This choice cut of beef is always tender and cooks in minutes. Here, the steaks are seared with shallots and the pan juices are deglazed to make a tasty sauce, and then they are served with roasted red potatoes topped with tangy melted Roquefort cheese. Sautéed spinach, accented with garlic and juicy orange segments, complements the rich meat and potatoes. Fresh strawberries and cubes of cool, succulent mango make a striking dessert combination—one that goes quite well with Champagne.

A classified Bordeaux adds opulence (try Carruades de Lafite, the second label of Château Lafite-Rothschild, or consider, at the higher end, Cos d'Estournel). Just as special are the finer California cabernets, such as Caymus or Flora Springs.

FILET MIGNON WITH SHALLOTS AND COGNAC
If you want to marinate the beef for longer than twenty minutes, cover it and place it in the refrigerator.

   2 6-ounce filet mignon steaks, about 1¼ inches thick
   ¼ cup cognac or other brandy
   ½ teaspoon fresh-ground black pepper
   1 tablespoon butter
   1 tablespoon cooking oil
   2 large shallots, minced
   ¼ cup beef stock or canned beef broth
       Salt

1. Sprinkle the steaks with 1 tablespoon of the cognac and let stand at room temperature for 20 minutes.

2. Rub the steaks on both sides with the pepper. In a heavy medium frying pan, melt ½ tablespoon of the butter with ½ tablespoon of the oil over high heat. When the pan is very hot, add the steaks, cover partially and cook until a crust forms on the bottom, about 2 minutes. Turn the steaks over and cook, partially covered, until crusted on the other side, about 2 minutes. Continue cooking over moderate heat until done to your taste, turning once, about 2 minutes per side for medium rare. Transfer the steaks to a plate and keep warm.

3. Melt the remaining ½ tablespoon butter with the remaining ½ tablespoon oil in the pan. Add the shallots; cook over moderately high heat, stirring frequently, until translucent, about 3 minutes.

4. Add the remaining 3 tablespoons cognac to the pan. Ignite with a match and cook over high heat until the flame burns out, about 30 seconds. Add the stock and boil until the liquid in the pan is reduced to ¼ cup, 2 to 3 minutes. Stir in any accumulated juices from the steaks.

5. Season the steaks with salt and transfer to individual plates. Spoon the pan sauce on top and serve.

—BOB CHAMBERS

OVEN-ROASTED RED POTATOES WITH ROQUEFORT
Société-brand Roquefort is one of the best, but you can also try other blue cheeses made from sheep's milk.

  1 tablespoon olive oil
  ½ pound small red potatoes, halved
  ¼ teaspoon salt
  ¼ teaspoon fresh-ground black pepper
2½ ounces Roquefort, crumbled (about ⅔ cup)

1. Heat the oven to 450°. Brush the oil on a nonstick baking sheet. Arrange the potatoes, cut-side up, on the baking sheet. Sprinkle with the salt and pepper and turn the potatoes over.

GAME PLAN

Marinate the beef.

Hull the strawberries.

Dice the mango and chill.

Bake the potatoes.

Prepare the ingredients for the filet mignon and spinach; cook both these dishes no more than 10 minutes before serving.

Combine the strawberries and diced mango just before serving dessert.

2. Roast the potatoes for about 20 minutes, until browned on the bottom. Turn them over and keep warm. Leave the oven on.

3. Five minutes before serving, sprinkle the cheese on the potatoes. Bake about 3 minutes, until the cheese starts to melt. Do not overcook or the cheese will melt off the potatoes.

—BOB CHAMBERS

SAUTÉED SPINACH WITH GARLIC AND ORANGE

Fresh spinach is always a luxury, particularly when someone else does the stemming and cleaning; look for prewashed to save time.

1 navel orange
1 tablespoon butter
1 clove garlic, minced
1 pound spinach, stems removed and leaves washed
   Salt and fresh-ground black pepper

1. Using a knife, peel the orange, removing all the white pith. Cut between the membranes to release the segments; halve them crosswise.

2. Melt the butter in a medium stainless-steel saucepan. Add the garlic and cook over moderately high heat, stirring, until fragrant, about 2 minutes. Add the spinach and toss to coat. Cover and cook until the spinach is wilted, about 2 minutes. Drain off any liquid and season with salt and pepper. Gently stir in the orange segments and serve.

—BOB CHAMBERS

SCALLOPS MEET SHIITAKES

Working under the assumption that it is silly to wait in line at your favorite fishmonger's to buy only one item, we present two seafood dishes in this menu—a shrimp-and-avocado first course, followed by scallops and mushrooms in the main course. The sweet bay scallops and woodsy shiitake mushrooms are an unexpected yet delightful pairing.

For dessert, try a sophisticated spin-off of the ice cream sandwich. Instead of bland vanilla ice cream between two plain cookies, we have a blend of luscious mascarpone cheese, bittersweet chocolate, and coffee liqueur sandwiched between imported *gaufrettes*.

Mushrooms call for an earthy white, but one with subtlety, so that the scallops are not lost in the shuffle. Try a white Bordeaux from Entre-Deux-Mers, where oak is less abundantly used, or a white Rioja.

SHRIMP AND AVOCADO WITH MUSTARD VINAIGRETTE

It is close to impossible to find a perfectly ripened avocado at the super-market. We suggest buying an underripe one on the weekend and letting it ripen over the course of two or three days.

1½ tablespoons wine vinegar
1½ tablespoons Dijon mustard
¼ cup olive oil
   Salt and fresh-ground black pepper
½ pound medium shrimp, shelled
1 ripe avocado, preferably Hass, halved lengthwise, pitted and peeled
2 tablespoons diced fresh tomato (optional)
2 tablespoons minced fresh chives

1. In a small glass or stainless-steel bowl, whisk together the vinegar and mustard. Slowly whisk in the oil. Season the vinaigrette with salt and pepper.

2. In a small saucepan of boiling water, cook the shrimp until just opaque, about 1 minute. Drain.

3. Set the avocado halves on plates. Spoon the shrimp into the avocado halves and drizzle with the vinaigrette. Top with the tomato, if using, and chives.

—AMY FARGES

BAY SCALLOPS WITH SAUTÉED SHIITAKES

1½ tablespoons butter
½ pound shiitake mushrooms, stems discarded and caps sliced
1 tablespoon minced shallot
Salt and fresh-ground black pepper
½ pound bay scallops
1 cup packed small spinach leaves
2 tablespoons diced fresh tomato (optional)
1 tablespoon minced fresh chives

1. In a large stainless-steel frying pan, melt the butter over moderate heat. Add the shiitakes and shallot and cook, stirring, until wilted, about 5 minutes. Season with salt and pepper.

2. Add the scallops to the pan and cook until opaque, about 2 minutes. Add the spinach and stir to wilt. Add the tomato and season again. Top with the chives and serve.

—AMY FARGES

BITTERSWEET CHOCOLATE CREAM SANDWICHES
Mascarpone cheese lends incomparable richness to the filling. The recipe makes four sandwiches, just in case you want seconds on dessert.

¼ cup heavy cream
1 ounce bittersweet chocolate
½ cup mascarpone cheese

GAME PLAN

Prepare the chocolate cream.

Steam the rice.

Make the vinaigrette.

Cook the shrimp.

Assemble the chocolate cream sandwiches.

Assemble the first course.

Prepare the scallops and shiitakes.

1 tablespoon sugar
1 teaspoon coffee liqueur
8 large imported waffle cookies (*gaufrettes*)

1. In a small saucepan, scald the cream over moderate heat. Add the chocolate and remove from the heat. Let stand until melted, about 3 minutes. Stir until smooth.

2. In a bowl, whisk the mascarpone until fluffy. Whisk in the sugar, liqueur, and chocolate cream. Refrigerate for 15 minutes, until firm.

3. Spread 4 of the waffle cookies with the chilled chocolate cream, top with the remaining 4 cookies and refrigerate.

—AMY FARGES

MAHIMAHI AND MORE

A really fresh piece of fish needs very little dressing up. A splash of balsamic vinegar, a scattering of capers, and some butter are all it takes to create a sophisticated main course. In keeping with the spirit of this meal, the vegetables should be kept simple as well. Here, new potatoes and carrots are cooked until just tender and tossed with a bit of butter. If you choose mâche (a.k.a. lamb's lettuce or lambs' tongues) for your salad green, you only need to dress the dark green leaves with a few drops of fruity olive oil and a squeeze of lemon juice.

The luscious pudding should be made well before dinner because it needs some time to chill in the refrigerator. Everything else is cooked quickly at the last minute.

The richness of the mahimahi suggests a match with an equally rich but lively white wine. Seek out a California viognier (such as R.H. Phillips EXP), or a *dry* gewürztraminer from Oregon.

BROILED MAHIMAHI WITH BUTTERY CAPER SAUCE
If mahimahi is not available, flounder, sole, cod, or even pompano works well in this easy recipe.

12 ounces skinless mahimahi fillet, cut into 2 equal pieces
    Salt and fresh-ground black pepper
2 tablespoons butter
1 teaspoon balsamic vinegar
1 teaspoon drained capers
2 teaspoons minced flat-leaf parsley

1. Heat the broiler. Line a large rimmed baking sheet or a broiler pan with aluminum foil. Set the mahimahi in the pan and broil about 6 inches from the heat for 3 to 5 minutes, or until firm and just opaque throughout. Season with the salt and pepper.

2. In a small saucepan, melt the butter over moderately low heat. Add the vinegar and capers and cook until heated through, about 1 minute. Remove from the heat and stir in the parsley. Spoon over each fillet and serve.

—ANNE WALSH

ABOUT MAHIMAHI

An increasingly popular fish, mahimahi is caught in the warm waters off Hawaii, California, and Florida. The dark flesh turns pearly white when cooked and has a firm texture with a large flake. The flavor is mild without being bland. Always skin mahimahi fillets before cooking. When purchasing, avoid fillets that are brown and streaky, a sign that the fish is not absolutely fresh.

NEW POTATOES AND CARROTS WITH DILL

If you cannot find fresh dill, substitute fresh mint.

8 small new potatoes, scrubbed and halved
2 medium carrots, sliced on the diagonal into 1-inch pieces
1 tablespoon butter, at room temperature
1½ teaspoons chopped fresh dill
   Salt and fresh-ground black pepper

1. Put the potatoes in a saucepan, cover with cold salted water, and bring to a boil over high heat. Add the carrot slices and cook, stirring occasionally, until the potatoes are tender when pierced with a fork, about 10 minutes.

2. Drain the vegetables and return to the saucepan. Add the butter, dill, salt, and pepper. Toss to coat well. Serve immediately.

—ANNE WALSH

GAME PLAN

Make the pudding and chill.

Heat the broiler.

Scrub and slice the potatoes and the carrots; put on to boil.

Wash and spin-dry the salad greens.

Broil the fish; prepare the sauce.

Dress the greens.

RICOTTA PUDDING

This purely wonderful dessert could also be served with fresh berries.

    1   cup (8 ounces) ricotta
    ¼   cup heavy cream
    ¼   cup confectioners' sugar
    ½   teaspoon grated orange zest
    2   drops vanilla extract
        Cinnamon or grated nutmeg, for garnish

In a food processor, combine the ricotta, cream, confectioners' sugar, orange zest, and vanilla. Process until smooth and creamy. Spoon the mixture into bowls or wineglasses and chill for about 30 minutes or up to 4 hours. Sprinkle a pinch of cinnamon or nutmeg over each pudding and serve cold.

—MARIE SIMMONS

SNAPPER IN SAKE

In this light, Japanese-style menu, the snapper fillets take less than five minutes to cook in a mixture of sake, soy sauce, and mirin, a sweet rice wine. The broccoli is accented with garlic and red-pepper flakes, and the cucumber salad is seasoned very simply with rice-wine vinegar, a little salt, and sesame seeds. Steamed medium-grain white rice is the perfect foil for the distinctive flavors in this meal.

Consider sake, since you will have a good deal left over from the recipe. Other possibilities: Verdicchio dei Castelli di Jesi, with fresh herb flavors and zippy acidity, will work well. For something tonier, try a Sancerre from Lucien Crochet.

BRAISED SNAPPER WITH SAKE AND SOY SAUCE

Look for mirin at Asian markets, health-food stores, and large supermarkets. If it is unavailable, substitute the same amount of dry sherry and increase the sugar to one teaspoon.

2 red-snapper fillets with skin (about 6 ounces each)
⅓ cup sake (Japanese rice wine)
2 tablespoons mirin (sweet Japanese cooking wine)
2 tablespoons soy sauce
1 tablespoon peeled, slivered fresh ginger
½ teaspoon sugar
1 scallion, green part only, cut into thin slices on the diagonal

1. With a sharp, thin-bladed knife, make 3 shallow slashes through the skin of the fillets to keep them from curling.

2. In a frying pan, combine the sake, mirin, soy sauce, ginger, and

sugar and bring to a simmer over high heat. Add the fish, skin-side up, in a single layer. Cover and simmer over moderate heat until just cooked through, about 4 minutes. Transfer the fillets to large plates, spoon the sauce on top, and sprinkle with the scallion greens.

—STEPHANIE LYNESS

BROCCOLI WITH SPICY SESAME OIL

¾ pound broccoli florets
2 teaspoons Asian sesame oil
1 small clove garlic, minced
  Dried red-pepper flakes
1 teaspoon soy sauce
½ teaspoon lemon juice

1. Bring a large pot of salted water to a boil. Add the broccoli and cook until just tender, about 1 minute. Drain.

2. In a large frying pan, warm the sesame oil, garlic, and red-pepper flakes over low heat for 3 minutes. Stir in the soy sauce and lemon juice. Add the broccoli, toss to coat, and serve.

—STEPHANIE LYNESS

CUCUMBER SALAD WITH RICE-WINE VINEGAR

1 teaspoon sesame seeds
1 cucumber, peeled in strips lengthwise, leaving stripes of skin, halved lengthwise, seeded, and sliced
½ teaspoon rice-wine vinegar
  Salt

1. In a small frying pan, toast the sesame seeds over moderate heat until lightly browned, about 1 minute. Set aside.

2. In a medium serving bowl, toss the cucumber slices with the rice-wine vinegar and salt to taste. Cover and refrigerate for 30 to 40 minutes. Sprinkle with the sesame seeds just before serving.

—STEPHANIE LYNESS

GAME PLAN

Make the cucumber salad.

Cook the rice.

Slice the pineapple for dessert.

Prepare the broccoli.

Pan-braise the snapper fillets.

CASUAL CHIC

Two chicken breasts, one portobello mushroom the size of a saucer, a little wine, and some cream are all you need to make a satisfying main course for two. The vegetable-hash accompaniment—a very, very distant cousin of the old red-flannel hash—plays off the crispness of roasted potatoes against the tenderness of sautéed fennel punctuated with fresh thyme and parsley. Fresh strawberries with a balsamic-vinegar glaze are served over ice cream for dessert.

White Graves, from Bordeaux, is a classic blend of lively sauvignon blanc and oily sémillon. The result is a seductively textured wine with balanced acid and some oak nuances—which adds up to a wonderful match for this dish. Similar blends are available from Washington State as well.

CHICKEN WITH PORTOBELLO MUSHROOM SAUCE
The dark, meaty portobello is a cultivated mushroom; exotic-looking, it is, in fact, a common brown or cremini mushroom that has been permitted to grow a few more days.

 1 large portobello mushroom, stem removed
 2 teaspoons olive oil
    Salt and fresh-ground black pepper
 2 boneless chicken breasts with skin
 ¼ cup dry white wine
 2 tablespoons chicken stock or canned low-sodium chicken broth
 2 tablespoons heavy cream

1. Heat the oven to 425°. Set the mushroom, stemmed-side

down, in a metal pie plate. Brush the mushroom with ½ teaspoon of the oil and season with salt and pepper. Roast for about 12 minutes, or until tender. Cut the mushroom into thin slices and transfer to a plate.

2. Heat the remaining 1½ teaspoons oil in a medium stainless-steel frying pan. Season the chicken breasts on both sides with salt and pepper and place in the pan, skin-side down. Cook over moderately high heat, turning once, until well browned, about 5 minutes. Transfer to the plate with the mushrooms. Pour off the fat from the pan. Return the chicken to the pan, lower the heat to moderate, cover, and cook until opaque throughout, about 5 minutes longer. Transfer the chicken to a plate and keep warm.

3. Add the wine to the frying pan and boil over high heat, stirring to scrape up any brown bits, until reduced by half, about 3 minutes. Add the stock and reduce by half, about 1 minute. Add the cream and continue boiling until reduced by half, about 1 minute more. Stir in the sliced mushrooms and season with salt and pepper. Set each chicken breast on a large plate and spoon the sauce over the top.

—NICO MARTIN

ROASTED RED-POTATO-AND-FENNEL HASH

½ pound small unpeeled red potato,
   cut into ½-inch-thick slices
1 teaspoon olive oil
   Salt and fresh-ground black pepper
2 teaspoons butter
1 small bulb fennel, trimmed, cored and cut crosswise into
   thin slices
½ teaspoon chopped fresh thyme
2 teaspoons chopped flat-leaf parsley

1. Heat the oven to 425°. Spread the potato slices in a single layer on a lightly oiled baking sheet. Drizzle the oil over the potatoes and season with salt and pepper. Roast for about 45 minutes, until browned and crisp.

GAME PLAN

Heat the oven to 350°.

Macerate the strawberries, toast the walnuts, and make the balsamic glaze.

Roast and slice the mushroom; roast the potatoes; slice and sauté the fennel.

Brown the chicken.

Make the mushroom sauce.

Toss the potatoes with the fennel.

2. Meanwhile, melt the butter in a large frying pan. Add the fennel and cook over moderate heat, stirring frequently, until tender, about 15 minutes. Stir in the thyme.

3. Just before serving, add the potatoes and parsley to the fennel and stir quickly over high heat until warmed through. Season the hash with salt and pepper and serve.

—NICO MARTIN

ICE CREAM WITH STRAWBERRIES AND BALSAMIC-VINEGAR GLAZE

Balsamic vinegar, tempered with brown sugar and reduced to a glaze, makes a surprisingly sweet, tangy topping for the ice cream and berries.

½ pint strawberries, hulled and quartered
1 teaspoon granulated sugar
¼ cup chopped walnuts
½ cup balsamic vinegar
1½ tablespoons dark brown sugar
    Pinch cinnamon
    Tiny pinch ground cloves
    Tiny pinch ground allspice
    Vanilla ice cream

1. In a small bowl, sprinkle the strawberries with the granulated sugar. Let stand at room temperature for 30 minutes.

2. Heat the oven to 350°. Spread the walnuts in a metal pie plate and toast for about 7 minutes, or until fragrant. Let cool slightly, then chop.

3. In a stainless-steel saucepan, combine the vinegar, brown sugar, cinnamon, cloves, and allspice. Bring to a boil over high heat and cook until reduced to 2 tablespoons, 5 to 7 minutes. Pour into a cup and refrigerate until chilled.

4. Scoop ice cream into two bowls. Top with the strawberries and drizzle with the balsamic glaze. Top with the chopped nuts and serve.

—NICO MARTIN

HERB-ROASTED CORNISH HENS

When time is tight and you want an oven-roasted bird, Cornish hens are the answer. These hens are stuffed under the skin with an aromatic mixture of garlic, fresh herbs, and olive oil that flavors the meat and keeps it moist. Drizzling the birds with fresh lemon juice after they come out of the oven brightens their taste.

An uncomplicated pea soup opens the meal; its aromatic garden-fresh garnish of mint and sorrel lifts the recipe well above the ordinary. Serve the hens with crusty French bread and greens that are tossed with our tart goat-cheese dressing. For dessert, we suggest a tropical-fruit sorbet.

The delicate flavors and aromas in this meal necessitate a subdued wine to avoid unwanted clashes. Northern Italian whites, like soave or a pinot bianco, have light flavors and aromas, along with the necessary palate-cleansing acidity.

SPRING PEA SOUP WITH SORREL

The flavor of sorrel is not unlike spinach with a lemony zing.

1 teaspoon cooking oil
2 shallots, minced
1 sprig thyme
2 tablespoons dry white wine
2 cups shelled fresh peas (about 2 pounds in the pod)
   or one 10-ounce package frozen petite peas, thawed
1¼ cups water
   Salt and fresh-ground black pepper
   Several fresh sorrel leaves, torn into pieces
1 tablespoon chopped fresh mint leaves

1. Heat the oil in a medium stainless-steel saucepan. Add the shallots and thyme, cover, and cook over low heat, stirring once, for 5 minutes. Add the wine and simmer for 1 minute. Add the peas and water and bring to a boil over high heat. Cover and cook over low heat until the peas are just tender, 5 to 8 minutes for fresh peas, 3 to 4 minutes for frozen.

2. Puree the soup in a food processor or blender. Pass through a strainer into a bowl, pressing down on the solids.

3. Return the soup to the saucepan. Season with salt and pepper and bring to a simmer over moderately high heat. Stir the sorrel and mint into the soup just before serving.

—MARCIA KIESEL

ROAST CORNISH HENS WITH MIXED HERBS AND LEMON

Feel free to vary the herb mix according to your personal taste—and what you have in the herb garden.

1 clove garlic, minced
2 tablespoons minced flat-leaf parsley
2 teaspoons chopped fresh thyme
1 teaspoon chopped fresh sage
3 tablespoons olive oil
½ teaspoon salt
½ teaspoon fresh-ground black pepper
2 Cornish hens (about 1 pound each)
Juice of 1 lemon

1. Heat oven to 450°. In a small bowl, combine the garlic with the parsley, thyme, and sage. Stir in the oil, salt, and pepper.

2. Loosen the breast skin of each hen with your fingers. Spread about 1 tablespoon of the herb mixture under the skin of each bird, rubbing it over the breast and thighs. Rub the hens with the remaining herb mixture and transfer to a baking dish.

3. Roast the hens in the lower third of the oven for 20 minutes, basting once or twice. Reduce the oven temperature to 300° and

GAME PLAN

Heat the oven.

Blend the fresh herb garnish and rub the Cornish hens with it: roast the hens.

Mix the salad dressing and wash the lettuce.

Shell the peas and make the pea soup.

continue roasting the birds for 15 to 20 minutes longer, basting occasionally, until the juices run clear when a thigh is pierced with a skewer.

4. Transfer the hens to a platter and drizzle with the lemon juice. Cover the birds loosely with aluminum foil and let stand for about 5 minutes before serving.

—BOB CHAMBERS

TANGY GOAT CHEESE DRESSING

  2 ounces soft goat cheese, at room temperature
  1 teaspoon wine vinegar
½ teaspoon Dijon mustard
     Pinch superfine sugar
  1 tablespoon buttermilk
  1 tablespoon water, more if needed
     Salt and fresh-ground white pepper
1½ teaspoons minced scallion

1. In a small bowl, stir the goat cheese, vinegar, mustard, and sugar until smooth. Stir in the buttermilk and water until smooth; if necessary, stir in a few drops more water. Season with salt and pepper. Stir in the scallion just before serving.

—GRACE PARISI

Summer

New World Pappardelle (p. 145)

Seafood Salad (p. 143)

STEAK SALAD
TONIGHT

You ran by the butcher's counter and picked up the makings of a quick meal: flavorful rib or boneless rib-eye steaks, or tender shell or boneless strip steaks. How can you make this week's steak dinner different from last week's? A steak salad provides a welcome change, particularly one that combines lightly wilted bitter greens, Roquefort, and walnuts. Oniony mashed potatoes make a tasty side dish. The rich meal calls for a light finish—sorbet garnished with fresh fruit.

On a hot evening, you can safely break the rules and have an intense white wine—a New Zealand sauvignon blanc or an Australian sémillon. Or in a red, try a light herbaceous cabernet franc, such as a Chinon or Bourgueil from the Loire Valley in France.

MARINATED-STEAK SALAD
If you do not have walnut oil, substitute olive oil.

- 1 small shallot, minced
- ¼ teaspoon minced fresh rosemary
- ¼ teaspoon salt
- ¼ teaspoon fresh-ground black pepper
- 1½ tablespoons sherry vinegar
- 1 tablespoon Dijon mustard
- 2 tablespoons walnut oil
- 3 tablespoons cooking oil
- 2 1-inch-thick boneless beef steaks (about 7 ounces each)
- ¼ cup chopped walnuts
- 1 head Belgian endive, sliced into 1-inch pieces
- ½ pound escarole, torn into 2-inch pieces
- 2 ounces Roquefort, crumbled (about ½ cup)

1. In a small stainless-steel saucepan, combine the shallot, rosemary, salt, and pepper. Stir in the vinegar and mustard. Whisk in the walnut oil and cooking oil. Pour ¼ cup of the dressing into a shallow glass baking dish, add the steaks, and turn to coat. Set aside to marinate for 30 minutes.

2. Meanwhile, heat the oven to 350°. Toast the walnuts for about 3 minutes, or until fragrant.

3. Light the grill. Grill the steaks until done to your taste, about 2 minutes per side for medium rare. Let rest for 2 minutes.

4. Warm the remaining dressing over low heat. Toss the endive, escarole, Roquefort, and walnuts with the dressing and mound on two plates. Cut each steak diagonally across the grain into five slices and arrange on the salads.

—PAUL GRIMES

> ## ABOUT WALNUT OIL
> Walnut oil imparts an unmistakable roasted-nut flavor to salads. It is an expensive product, made by age-old methods. Shelled walnuts are ground to a paste, and the paste is slowly heated to release the oil, which is then extracted by pressing. Like all nut oils, walnut oil is quite perishable. Buy it in small quantities, store it in the refrigerator, and always taste a little before adding to a recipe to make sure the oil has not gone rancid.

GAME PLAN

Marinate the steak; prepare the salad ingredients.

Light the grill.

Boil the potatoes and brown the onions.

Prepare the berries.

Grill the steaks.

Mash the potatoes.

Assemble the salad.

MASHED POTATOES WITH BROWNED ONIONS

1 pound potatoes, scrubbed and cubed
   Salt
3 tablespoons butter
1 small onion, minced
½ cup hot milk
   Fresh-ground black pepper

1. Put potatoes in a medium saucepan, cover with water, and add 1 teaspoon salt. Bring to a boil over moderate heat and cook until tender, about 15 minutes. Drain and return to the pan to keep warm.

2. Meanwhile, melt 2 tablespoons of the butter in a frying pan. Add the onion and cook, stirring occasionally, over moderately low heat until well browned, about 15 minutes.

3. Mash the potatoes with the milk and the remaining 1 tablespoon butter. Stir in the onion. Season to taste with salt and pepper.

—PAUL GRIMES

LEMON SORBET WITH RASPBERRIES AND CASSIS

Chambord liqueur is a good substitute for crème de cassis.

- ½ cup raspberries
- ½ teaspoon grated lemon zest
- ¼ teaspoon sugar
- 2 tablespoons crème de cassis (black currant liqueur)
  Lemon sorbet

1. In a medium bowl, toss the raspberries with the lemon zest and sugar. Let sit for 5 minutes. Stir in the cassis and set aside for at least 10 minutes.

2. Scoop the sorbet into two dessert bowls. Spoon the raspberries and cassis on top and serve immediately.

—SUSAN SHAPIRO JASLOVE

A LITTLE MEXICAN FEAST

Here is a light and flavorful authentic Mexican dinner that is ready in under an hour—with the help of a neat short-cut. The timesaving trick is used in making the sumptuous main course of sautéed chicken breasts baked with poblano sauce. For the rich, creamy sauce, the chile is fried until the skin is tender and then pureed. This eliminates the time-consuming step of roasting and peeling the pepper.

To accompany the chicken, there is white rice with corn kernels and onion. Serve a sweet and spicy mango salad, dressed with orange juice and sprinkled with lime-marinated onion and serrano chile, along with the chicken and rice. Strawberry ice cream makes a cooling dessert.

The richness of creamy Monterey jack and sour cream needs an acidic counterpoint from the wine. A Gavi, with its typical acidity and mineral accents, has what it takes to keep the feast lively.

CHICKEN BREASTS IN POBLANO SAUCE
Cooking the poblano chile before incorporating it into the sauce brings out the pepper's complex, robust flavor.

2 tablespoons butter
1 large poblano chile, seeded and sliced into ¼-inch strips
1 small onion, cut into ¼-inch-thick slices
2 boneless, skinless chicken breasts (about 6 ounces each)
  Salt and fresh-ground black pepper
¼ cup sour cream
¼ cup milk
¼ pound Monterey jack, grated (about 1⅓ cups)

1. Heat the oven to 350°. Melt 1 tablespoon of the butter in a medium frying pan. Add the poblano and onion and cook over moderate heat, stirring, until softened, about 10 minutes.

2. Meanwhile, melt the remaining 1 tablespoon butter in a large heavy frying pan. Season the chicken breasts with salt and pepper and add them, rounded-side down, to the pan. Cook over moderately high heat until browned, about 5 minutes per side. Place the chicken breasts in a baking dish.

3. Transfer the cooked poblano mixture to a blender with the sour cream and milk; puree until smooth. Season with salt and pepper. Pour the sauce over the chicken and sprinkle the cheese on top. Bake for about 25 minutes, until the sauce is bubbling and the chicken is cooked through.

—CHATA DuBOSE

RICE PILAF WITH CORN

To thaw the corn quickly, put the frozen kernels in a colander under cool running water or stick them in the microwave. The moist pilaf can stand for up to twenty minutes after cooking, if desired.

1 teaspoon cooking oil
½ cup long-grain rice
2 tablespoons minced onion
1 clove garlic, minced
1 cup plus 2 tablespoons chicken stock
  or canned low-sodium chicken broth
1 cup frozen corn kernels, thawed
  Salt and fresh-ground black pepper

1. Heat the oil in a medium saucepan. Add the rice and stir over moderately high heat until toasted, 1 to 2 minutes. Add the onion and garlic and stir over moderately low heat for 2 minutes. Stir in the stock and bring to a boil over moderately high heat. Cover and cook over low heat for 10 minutes.

2. Stir the corn and ¼ teaspoon of salt into the rice. Cover and cook until the rice is tender, about 10 minutes longer. Remove

GAME PLAN

Start the salad by marinating the onion and slicing and soaking the mangos.

Heat the oven.

Sauté the poblanos and the chicken. Make the sauce.

Cook the rice.

Bake the chicken.

Finish the mango salad.

from the heat, season with salt and pepper, and serve.

—CHATA DuBOSE

SAVORY MANGO SALAD

A ripe or slightly green mango can be used here. Soaking the mango in salted water heightens its flavor.

  2 tablespoons minced onion
1½ tablespoons lime juice
  1 large mango
  1 cup water
  ½ teaspoon salt
  ½ cup orange juice (from about 1 orange)
  1 medium serrano chile or jalapeño pepper, seeded and minced
     Fresh cilantro leaves

1. In a small bowl, toss the onion with the lime juice. Let stand for 40 minutes.

2. Meanwhile, score the mango skin into quarters. Peel half the mango and cut ¼-inch-lengthwise slices down to the pit. Cut crosswise to release the slices. Repeat with the other side. In a large bowl, combine the water with the salt. Add the mango slices and let stand for 40 minutes.

3. Drain the mango and pat dry. Transfer to a bowl and add the orange juice. Drain the onion and sprinkle over the mango with the chopped chile. Top with the cilantro.

—CHATA DuBOSE

BARBECUED CHICKEN SUPPER

Barbecued chicken is surely one of the best joys of summer. For the easy barbecue sauce, we use tomato paste rather than ketchup to cut back on the sweetness. Molasses is added to deepen the flavor, and hot-pepper sauce contributes heat; feel free to adjust the quantity to suit your taste. A thyme-scented potato salad and fresh-from-the-garden beans round out the supper. For dessert, dress up plain vanilla ice cream with some orange zest and crystallized ginger, then scoop it into bowls and top with fresh berries. Any leftover chicken will be ideal for a weekend lunch or picnic.

A barbecue on a warm summer night is not well served by a heavy wine, yet the wine needs enough body to match the sauce's deep flavor. The simple fruit of a barbera will not let you down nor, if you desire a little more body, will a Côtes-du-Rhône.

BARBECUED CHICKEN

This recipe makes more sauce than you will need for one chicken. Refrigerate or freeze half of it for later use on pork chops or ribs.

  1 tablespoon cooking oil
  1 small onion, minced
  1 clove garlic, minced
  1 can (6 ounces) tomato paste
 ⅓ cup molasses
 ¼ cup plus 2 tablespoons white vinegar
  2 tablespoons Dijon mustard
1½ teaspoons sugar
1½ teaspoons hot-pepper sauce
  1 teaspoon paprika

  1 teaspoon salt
½ teaspoon ground ginger
1¼ cups water
  1 chicken (about 2½ pounds), cut in 8 pieces

1. Light the grill or heat the broiler. In a medium stainless-steel saucepan, heat the oil over moderately low heat. Add the onion and cook, stirring, until softened, about 3 minutes. Add the garlic and cook for 1 minute longer. Stir in the tomato paste, molasses, vinegar, mustard, sugar, hot-pepper sauce, paprika, salt, ginger, and water. Cover partially, increase the heat to moderate, and simmer until the sauce has thickened, about 20 minutes. (*The sauce can be made up to 1 week ahead; pour it into an airtight container and refrigerate. Or, freeze it for longer storage.*)

2. Place the chicken pieces away from the hottest part of the grill, cover, and grill, turning two or three times, until almost cooked through, about 30 minutes. Alternatively, broil the chicken, turning, for about 25 minutes. Brush on the sauce and grill or broil the chicken, turning and basting with the sauce two or three more times, until the juices run clear, 10 to 15 minutes longer.

—STEPHANIE LYNESS

WARM POTATO SALAD WITH THYME
Adding the wine and thyme to the potatoes while they are still hot helps the flavors penetrate deeply.

  1 pound small new potatoes
    Salt
½ tablespoon dry white wine
  1 teaspoon chopped fresh thyme, or
    ¼ teaspoon dried thyme
  1 tablespoon wine vinegar
½ teaspoon Dijon mustard
    Fresh-ground black pepper
  3 tablespoons olive oil
    Chopped scallion, for serving

GAME PLAN

Light the grill.

Cook the potatoes.

Make the barbecue sauce.

Grill the chicken.

Steam the beans.

Transfer the ice cream from the freezer to the refrigerator to soften.

1. Place the potatoes in a medium saucepan and add enough water to cover by 1 inch. Salt the water and bring to a boil over moderately high heat. Reduce the heat to moderate and simmer the potatoes until tender, about 15 minutes. Drain well. While the potatoes are still hot, quarter or halve them, depending on their size. Transfer the potatoes to a serving bowl and toss gently with the wine and thyme.

2. In a small glass or stainless-steel bowl, whisk the vinegar with the mustard and season with salt and pepper to taste. Gradually whisk in the oil. Pour the dressing over the potatoes and toss gently to coat. Sprinkle the scallion on top and serve warm.

—STEPHANIE LYNESS

GINGERED ICE CREAM WITH BERRIES

½ pint vanilla ice cream
1½ teaspoons minced crystallized ginger
½ teaspoon grated orange zest
½ cup raspberries or other berries

1. Put the ice cream in the refrigerator until soft but not soupy, about 20 minutes.

2. Spoon the softened ice cream into a bowl. Mix in the crystallized ginger and orange zest.

3. Scoop the ice cream into two dessert dishes and sprinkle the berries on top. Serve at once.

—STEPHANIE LYNESS

PASTA WITH SICILIAN PESTO

For a change of pace from standard pesto, here is an unusual Sicilian version. It relies on sweet tomatoes to enhance the sauce's summery flavor, and it uses almonds in place of the traditional pine nuts, revealing the Arabic influence on the Sicilian kitchen. The pesto is easily made in the blender without sacrificing texture and without the inconvenience of trying to incorporate the tomatoes into the basil puree with a mortar and pestle.

Start the meal with an antipasto that contrasts meaty olives with crunchy celery in a spicy lemon dressing. Sliced fresh fennel can replace the celery to give a tasty anise kick to the salad. Breadsticks, preferably thin grissini, are a crisp accompaniment. A sophisticated and refreshing chilled melon soup finishes the meal.

Cross the Adriatic for a classical combination. A hearty red from Greece (Boutari is a good producer) will make a unique pairing with the pesto. Otherwise, choose southern Italian reds such as Salice Salentino or Sicily's own Regaleali.

OLIVE-AND-CELERY ANTIPASTO
If you like, omit the romaine and prosciutto and just nibble on the olives and breadsticks while you prepare the main course.

- ¼ pound plump Mediterranean black and green olives, such as Kalamata or Gaeta
- 2 ribs celery, sliced into ¼-inch-thick pieces
- 1 tablespoon olive oil
- 1½ teaspoons lemon juice
- ⅛ teaspoon dried red-pepper flakes
- 2 tablespoons minced flat-leaf parsley

2 romaine lettuce leaves
  Salt, if needed
2 thin slices of prosciutto (optional)
  Breadsticks, for serving

1. In a medium glass or stainless-steel bowl, toss the olives and celery with the oil, lemon juice, and red-pepper flakes. Add the parsley and toss again. Let marinate at room temperature for at least 15 minutes, stirring occasionally.

2. Place a romaine leaf on each of two plates. Season the antipasto with salt, if necessary, and spoon over the lettuce. Top each serving with a slice of prosciutto, if using, and serve with breadsticks.

—JUDITH SUTTON

LINGUINE WITH TOMATO PESTO

Cheese is not traditionally used in this pesto, but we have added a sprinkling of grated Parmesan at the table to please American palates.

¼ cup sliced almonds (about 1 ounce)
2 cloves garlic, smashed
3 tablespoons olive oil
½ teaspoon salt
  Fresh-ground black pepper
½ pound ripe tomatoes, cut into 1-inch chunks
¾ cup fresh basil leaves, plus small sprigs for garnish
½ pound dried linguine
  Grated Parmesan, for serving

1. In a blender, combine 3 tablespoons of the almonds, the garlic, oil, ½ teaspoon salt, and pepper to taste, and pulse until coarsely chopped. Add the tomatoes and process to a puree. Add ½ cup of the basil leaves and process until smooth. Slice the remaining ¼ cup basil by hand and set aside.

2. In a large pot of boiling, salted water, cook the linguine until just done, about 11 minutes. Drain the pasta, reserving ¼ cup of the pasta-cooking water separately. Return the pasta to the pot, toss with the pesto, and let stand for 1 minute.

GAME PLAN

Make and chill the soup (speed up the process by chilling it in a stainless-steel bowl rather than a glass one).

Put a pot of water on to boil for the pasta.

Make the antipasto and let it stand at room temperature.

Make the pesto sauce while you cook the pasta.

3. Toss the pasta with the reserved pasta-cooking water. Transfer to a large bowl or individual plates and top with the remaining 1 tablespoon sliced almonds, the sliced basil, and the basil sprigs. Serve the linguine immediately, passing the Parmesan separately at the table.

—Judith Sutton

CHILLED ORANGE CANTALOUPE SOUP

For the best flavor, be sure to choose a very ripe melon.

 1 ripe cantaloupe, peeled, seeded, and cut into large chunks
 3 tablespoons sugar, preferably superfine
 3 tablespoons fresh orange juice
 ¼ teaspoon grated orange zest
 1 tablespoon slivered fresh mint
 Sugar cookies (optional)

In a blender, combine the cantaloupe, sugar, orange juice, and orange zest and blend until smooth. Transfer to a large bowl and refrigerate until chilled (at least 45 minutes). Serve the cantaloupe soup in shallow bowls or large cups, topped with the mint and accompanied with the cookies, if desired.

—Judith Sutton

ZESTY VEAL SCALOPPINE

This menu satisfies a summer craving for something light and simple that keeps in-kitchen time to a minimum. Thin sautéed veal scallops with a butter-and-vermouth sauce are the main course. With the veal, serve a rice pilaf made with fresh summer herbs. A yellow tomato salad topped with basil and red onion marinated with sherry vinegar and a little sugar takes advantage of produce at the peak of the season. And for an easy dessert, slice some peaches or nectarines, toss with a bit of vodka, and serve with a scoop or two of vanilla ice cream.

Veal lends itself to a full-bodied white or a light to medium red. Finesse is the key, as big, bold wines will be too much for the palate. White Burgundy or an Oregon chardonnay are appropriate whites, and a lighter pinot noir is the red to choose.

VEAL SCALOPPINE WITH LEMON, BLACK PEPPER, AND VERMOUTH

The veal can easily be replaced by turkey scaloppine.

2 tablespoons butter
1 tablespoon cooking oil
½ pound veal scaloppine, pounded ¼ inch thick
½ teaspoon coarse-ground black pepper
¼ cup dry vermouth
1 tablespoon lemon juice
½ teaspoon grated lemon zest

1. Heat the oven to 200°. In a large nonstick frying pan, melt 1 tablespoon of the butter with the oil until almost smoking. Season

the veal scaloppine on both sides with the pepper and add to the pan. Cook over high heat until just browned, about 30 seconds per side. Transfer the scaloppine to a platter and keep warm in the oven.

2. Add the vermouth to the frying pan and cook over moderately high heat, scraping up the brown bits, until reduced by half, about 2 minutes. Add the lemon juice and zest and bring to a boil. Remove the pan from the heat and stir in the remaining 1 tablespoon butter until melted. Spoon the sauce over the scaloppine and serve.

—BOB CHAMBERS

RICE PILAF WITH FRESH HERBS

1	tablespoon olive oil
¼	cup minced onion
¾	cup long-grain rice
1½	cups water
½	teaspoon salt
⅛	teaspoon fresh-ground black pepper
3	tablespoons chopped mixed fresh herbs, such as flat-leaf parsley, thyme, and chervil
1	tablespoon chopped fresh tarragon

1. In a small heavy saucepan, heat the oil. Add the onion and cook over high heat, stirring frequently, until translucent and beginning to brown, 2 to 3 minutes. Add the rice and cook, stirring constantly, for 1 minute.

2. Add the water to the pan, stir in the salt and pepper, and bring to a boil. Reduce the heat to moderately low, cover, and simmer until the rice is tender and the liquid is absorbed, about 18 minutes. Stir in the chopped mixed herbs and the tarragon.

—BOB CHAMBERS

GAME PLAN

Cook the pilaf.

Slice the peaches or nectarines, toss with a little sugar and vodka and chill.

Heat the oven.

Prepare the tomato salad.

Brown the veal scaloppine and make the pan sauce.

A SMART TART

Running from the bakery to the cheese store to the green-grocer after a busy work day can make you too tired to cook once you get home. A menu whose ingredients all come from one place is a godsend. Whether your closest market is a 40,000-square-foot food emporium or a humble corner deli, you can easily find what you need for this menu, which uses ordinary items in a not-so-ordinary way. A ready-to-use pie crust encloses a mix of Mediterranean vegetables in the free-form tart. The simple salad uses mesclun, that wonderfully convenient mix of prewashed salad greens. And anisette toasts, though not remarkable on their own, make a crunchy, aromatic crumb topping on plums for dessert.

To avoid smothering the light tart, drink an Orvieto, or a less common Bianco di Custoza, from Italy. Either of these bracing, easy wines will keep the meal lively, and they are perfect for warm weather.

ROASTED-VEGETABLE TART

Feel free to vary the vegetables in the filling. Try Swiss chard or artichokes (frozen artichoke hearts are a great convenience food).

½ medium eggplant (about 12 ounces),
   cut into ¼-inch-thick slices
1 medium portobello mushroom, cap only,
   cut into ¼-inch-thick slices
1 medium shallot, sliced thin
1 small red bell pepper, diced
1 zucchini, cut crosswise into ¼-inch-thick slices
1 tablespoon olive oil

Salt and fresh-ground black pepper
2 ounces Roquefort or other blue cheese, crumbled
1½ ounces cream cheese, softened
1 large egg yolk
1 tablespoon grated Parmesan
1 prepared pie crust, not in a tin

1. Heat the oven to 450°. Line a baking sheet with aluminum foil.

2. In a roasting pan, toss the eggplant, mushroom, shallot, bell pepper, and zucchini with the oil and season with salt and pepper. Roast the vegetables for 12 to 14 minutes, stirring once or twice, until softened. Lower the oven temperature to 400°.

3. Using a hand-held electric mixer, beat the Roquefort and cream cheese together until smooth. Add the egg yolk and Parmesan; beat until blended.

4. Place the pie crust on the baking sheet, unfold, and pinch together any tears. Spread the cheese mixture out on the crust, leaving a 2-inch border of dough. Arrange the roasted vegetables on top. Fold the dough up to partially cover the filling, crimping to seal the edges. Bake for 20 to 25 minutes, or until golden. Serve the vegetable tart warm.

—GRACE PARISI

MIXED SALAD GREENS WITH SUN-DRIED TOMATO VINAIGRETTE

This recipe makes more dressing than you need, for two reasons: a smaller amount would be impractical to do in the blender and it's nice to have leftovers for another day.

5 fresh basil leaves
1 small shallot, halved
6 reconstituted sun-dried tomatoes or sun-dried tomatoes packed in oil
1 tablespoon balsamic vinegar
½ teaspoon Dijon mustard
⅓ cup water

GAME PLAN

Heat the oven.

Cut up the vegetables and roast them while you prepare the tart.

While the tart bakes, make the dressing.

Assemble the dessert.

Put the dessert in the oven when the vegetable tart is done.

3 tablespoons olive oil
4 ounces mixed salad greens
Salt and fresh-ground black pepper

In a blender, puree the basil, shallot, tomatoes, vinegar, mustard, and water until smooth. Blend in the oil. In a bowl, toss the salad greens with 2 or 3 tablespoons of the dressing. Season with salt and pepper; serve.

—GRACE PARISI

ITALIAN PLUM BETTY
Peaches or fresh figs also work well here.

1 pound Italian plums, pitted and cut into ¼-inch wedges
3 tablespoons sugar
1 tablespoon rum
2 large anisette toasts
1½ tablespoons unsalted butter, melted

1. Heat the oven to 400°. Generously butter a 9-inch-round or 8-inch-square glass or stainless-steel baking dish.

2. Toss the plums with the sugar and rum; arrange in the prepared dish in an even layer. With a rolling pin, crush the toasts in a bag to ¼-inch crumbs. (Or pulse in a food processor.) Toss the crumbs with the butter; scatter over the fruit.

3. Bake until the plums are soft and the top is golden, about 15 minutes. Serve warm or at room temperature.

—GRACE PARISI

SPICY WINGS (AND THINGS)

Buffalo wings may be America's favorite bar food, but that doesn't mean you have to head to your local pub whenever you have a yen for them. You can easily make similarly spicy chicken at home with even tastier results.

The wing section gives you the most succulent meat on the bird along with lots of crisp skin. Our simple recipe requires only splashes of hot-pepper sauce and balsamic vinegar for tangy heat. A variation of America's favorite salad—the Caesar—provides a lively accompaniment. The garlic bread here is baked in a paper bag, which might sound odd, but the paper absorbs the moisture created in the bag and produces a dry heat that yields an extra-crisp crust and a hot, moist center. Use the brown or white paper bag that the loaf comes in (but only if it is unwaxed), or substitute one of the narrow brown-paper bags used by liquor stores.

Peppery flavors in food need an echo in the wine that accompanies them, and Australian shiraz always pleases with its notable spice and deep fruit. A full-bodied California zinfandel would fit the same bill.

PEPPERY CHICKEN WINGS
Double or triple this recipe for a crowd.

- 2 pounds chicken wings
- 1 teaspoon balsamic vinegar
- 1 teaspoon olive oil
- 1 tablespoon hot-pepper sauce
  Salt and fresh-ground black pepper

Heat the oven to 500°. Lightly oil a large rimmed baking sheet and spread the chicken wings out on it. Drizzle the balsamic vinegar and the oil over the wings and toss lightly. Pour the hot-pepper sauce over the wings, season with salt and pepper, and toss again. Roast the wings for about 30 minutes on the top shelf of the oven, until well browned and crisp. Keep warm until serving.

—Marcia Kiesel

CAESAR SALAD WITH WALNUTS

Arugula adds a peppery bite to this salad, and toasted walnuts stand in for the standard garlic croutons.

¼ cup walnut halves (about 1 ounce)
1 small shallot, minced
1 small clove garlic, minced
1 anchovy fillet, mashed, plus ¼ teaspoon of the anchovy oil
1 tablespoon lemon juice
1 teaspoon Dijon mustard
  Salt and fresh-ground black pepper
2 tablespoons olive oil
2 cups 2-inch pieces of romaine lettuce
2 cups 2-inch pieces of arugula
2 tablespoons grated Parmesan

GAME PLAN

Heat the oven.

Season the chicken wings and bake. Toast the walnuts at the same time.

Prepare the greens and the Caesar salad dressing.

Make the garlic bread and bake it as soon as the wings are done.

Toss the salad.

1. Heat the oven to 500°. Spread the walnuts on a baking sheet and toast in the oven for about 6 minutes, or until golden brown. Transfer to a plate and let cool.

2. In a small glass or stainless-steel bowl, combine the shallot, garlic, anchovy and anchovy oil, lemon juice, mustard, and salt and pepper to taste. Using a fork, whisk in the olive oil until smooth.

3. Just before serving, combine the romaine and arugula in a salad bowl. Pour the dressing over the greens and toss well. Add the toasted nuts and the Parmesan. Toss again and serve.

—Marcia Kiesel

GARLIC BREAD IN A BAG

If you don't want to use a bag, toast the halves separately on an oven rack, buttered side up, until golden.

1 small clove garlic, minced
1 tablespoon butter, softened
½ loaf of Italian bread, preferably semolina, halved lengthwise
1 tablespoon grated Parmesan

Heat the oven to 450°. In a small bowl, blend the garlic with the butter. Spread each bread half with the garlic butter and sprinkle with the Parmesan. Sandwich the bread halves together and put the loaf in a paper bag. Fold the top closed and bake in the center of the oven for about 8 minutes, or until the bag darkens slightly and the bread feels crisp when pressed through the bag.

—MARCIA KIESEL

CHICKEN WITH BLACKBERRIES

This dinner relies on some of Spain's most characteristic ingredients: olive oil, garlic, saffron, and sherry vinegar. The main course is roasted chicken basted with a sweet-sour blackberry and brown-sugar sauce, an adaptation of a centuries-old Moorish dish. To accompany the chicken, serve rice flavored with saffron and pine nuts and a spinach-and-mushroom salad dressed with sherry vinaigrette. A simple dessert of cheese complemented by a semisweet oloroso sherry rounds out this summer meal. Look for Spanish cheeses such as Manchego, a mild sheep's-milk variety, and Cabrales, a Gorgonzola-like blue.

Chicken and red wine? In this case, certainly. Fruit requires a fruity wine, and an acidic white would clash with the berries that sweeten the chicken. Wines from Spain's Ribera del Duero possess the fruitiness to do the job.

CHICKEN WITH BLACKBERRIES AND BROWN SUGAR
Either mashed fresh blackberries or blackberry preserves can be used in the sauce. The berries make a slightly tarter sauce, while the preserves produce a sweeter and thicker one. Use whatever chicken parts you prefer, just so they're bone-in rather than boneless.

½ cup dry white wine
1½ pounds chicken pieces
2 teaspoons fresh thyme, or ¼ teaspoon dried thyme
½ teaspoon paprika
  Salt and fresh-ground black pepper
¼ cup chicken stock or canned low-sodium chicken broth
1 tablespoon light brown sugar

3 tablespoons mashed fresh blackberries or blackberry
preserves
1 clove garlic, minced
1½ tablespoons wine vinegar
½ teaspoon olive oil
⅛ teaspoon ground cumin
¼ cup fresh blackberries, for serving (optional)

1. Heat the oven to 375°. Pour ¼ cup of the wine into a large glass or stainless-steel baking dish. Arrange the chicken pieces in the dish skin-side up. Sprinkle with the thyme and ¼ teaspoon of the paprika. Season with salt and pepper. Bake for 35 minutes, adding the remaining ¼ cup wine and then the chicken stock to the pan as the juices evaporate; baste the chicken occasionally.

2. Meanwhile, in a small bowl, combine the brown sugar with the blackberries, garlic, vinegar, oil, cumin, and the remaining ¼ teaspoon paprika.

3. Spoon the blackberry mixture over the chicken and continue cooking for about 10 minutes, basting occasionally, until the juices run clear when the chicken is pierced with a fork. Transfer the chicken to a serving platter and cover loosely with aluminum foil.

4. Pour the cooking juices into a small stainless-steel saucepan and skim off any fat. Bring the juices to a boil over moderate heat and cook until reduced by half, about 2 minutes. Season the sauce with salt and pepper and spoon over the chicken. Top with the fresh blackberries, if using, and serve.

—PENELOPE CASAS

SAFFRON RICE WITH PINE NUTS

1 tablespoon butter
1 tablespoon minced onion
1 tablespoon pine nuts
¾ cup medium-grain rice, such as arborio
1 cup chicken stock or canned low-sodium chicken broth
½ cup water

GAME PLAN

Heat the oven.

Wash the spinach.

Bake the chicken and mix the ingredients for the blackberry sauce.

Make the rice.

Whisk the vinaigrette. Slice the mushrooms and assemble the salad.

1 tablespoon minced flat-leaf parsley
1 teaspoon fresh thyme, or ⅛ teaspoon dried thyme
  Pinch saffron threads, crumbled
¼ teaspoon salt

1. Heat the oven to 375°. Melt the butter in a medium oven-proof saucepan. Add the onion and pine nuts and cook over moderate heat, stirring occasionally, until the onion is softened, about 5 minutes.

2. Stir the rice into the onion mixture. Add the stock, water, parsley, thyme, saffron, and salt and bring to a boil over moderately high heat. Cover and bake in the oven for 15 minutes. Let the rice stand at room temperature, covered, for 5 to 10 minutes, then fluff with a fork before serving.

—PENELOPE CASAS

SPINACH-AND-MUSHROOM SALAD
WITH SHERRY VINAIGRETTE

2 teaspoons sherry vinegar or other wine vinegar
¼ teaspoon Dijon mustard
2 tablespoons olive oil
1 tablespoon minced flat-leaf parsley
1 small clove garlic, minced
1 teaspoon fresh thyme, or ⅛ teaspoon dried thyme
  Salt and fresh-ground black pepper
¾ pound spinach, stems removed, leaves washed and
  torn into 2-inch pieces
4 mushrooms, sliced

In a medium glass or stainless-steel bowl, whisk the vinegar and the mustard. Whisk in the oil, parsley, garlic, and thyme. Season with salt and pepper. Toss in the spinach and serve with the mushrooms scattered on top.

—PENELOPE CASAS

GRILLED TUNA AND SALAD

In this menu, both the main course (herbed tuna steaks) and the side dish (a bread salad loaded with fresh tomatoes) make use of the grill. The raspberry dessert requires little more effort than melting some chocolate and whipping a bit of cream.

The meatiness of tuna requires the power and finesse of a pinot noir. Find a Carneros pinot from California or, better yet, a Burgundy (such as a Pommard or a Gevrey-Chambertin).

GRILLED TUNA WITH ROSEMARY AND THYME
Swordfish or marlin steaks are delicious grilled in the same fashion.

1½ tablespoons olive oil
1½ teaspoons chopped fresh rosemary
 1 teaspoon chopped fresh thyme, plus extra sprigs for garnish
    (optional)
 2 6-ounce tuna steaks, cut about ¾ inch thick
    Fresh-ground black pepper
¼ teaspoon salt
    Lemon wedges, for serving

1. Light the grill. On a large plate, combine the oil, rosemary, and thyme. Add the tuna and season with pepper to taste; turn to coat. Marinate for up to 30 minutes, turning a few times.

2. Season both sides of the tuna steaks with the salt. Grill about 4 inches from the heat for about 3 minutes on each side, or until just pink in the center. Transfer the tuna to plates and serve with lemon wedges and thyme sprigs on the side.

—STEPHANIE LYNESS

GRILLED BREAD SALAD WITH GOAT CHEESE

This generous salad is made with grilled bread, goat cheese, tomatoes, and fennel. Other vegetables, such as eggplant, leeks, or mushrooms, can also be added.

2 medium tomatoes (about ¾ pound), cored, halved, and cut into ¼-inch-thick slices; juice and seeds reserved
½ small bulb fennel, halved and cut crosswise into thin slices
2 to 3 very thin slices red onion, rings separated
Several fresh basil leaves, torn into pieces
¼ cup crumbled goat cheese
2½ tablespoons wine vinegar
¼ cup olive oil
Salt and fresh-ground black pepper
2 thick slices white country-style or sourdough bread, crusts trimmed
1 clove garlic, halved

1. Light the grill. In a wide, shallow salad bowl, combine the tomatoes with their reserved juice and seeds and the fennel, onion, basil, and goat cheese. Add the vinegar and 2½ tablespoons of the oil. Season with salt and pepper and toss well.

2. Brush both sides of the bread slices with the remaining 1½ tablespoons oil. Grill about 4 inches from the heat for about 4 minutes on each side, or until golden brown. Rub the cut garlic over both sides of the grilled bread. Let the bread cool, then cut it into 1-inch squares. Add the bread to the salad bowl and toss. Serve immediately.

—STEPHANIE LYNESS

FRESH RASPBERRIES WITH CREAM AND CHOCOLATE

The technique of breaking a thin layer of hardened chocolate into slivers gives a professional chocolatier's touch to the dessert with very little effort.

½ ounce semisweet chocolate, chopped
½ cup heavy cream
1½ teaspoons confectioners' sugar
½ pint raspberries

GAME PLAN

Light the grill.

Marinate the tuna.

Prepare the salad ingredients.

Make the dessert.

Grill the bread and the tuna.

Assemble the salad.

1. Line a baking sheet with waxed paper. Melt the chocolate in a double boiler, stirring occasionally, until smooth. Alternatively, put the chocolate in a small microwaveable bowl. Melt in the microwave oven at medium power for 30 seconds. Stir and micro-wave for another 30 seconds, or until smooth.

2. Spread the chocolate as thinly as possible on the prepared baking sheet. Place in the freezer until hard, about 10 minutes.

3. Meanwhile, in a medium bowl, beat the cream until it holds soft peaks when the beaters are lifted. Add the confectioners' sugar and beat until firm peaks form.

4. Peel the chocolate off the waxed paper; break into pieces or chop with a knife into slivers.

5. Spoon the berries into two dessert dishes or wineglasses. Top with the whipped cream and garnish with the chocolate. Serve immediately or refrigerate for up to 30 minutes.

—STEPHANIE LYNESS

JAMAICAN CHICKEN IN A JIFFY

This summer menu relies on the microwave to reduce the time needed to marinate chicken before putting it on the grill, cutting it from several hours to just ten minutes. In the microwave, the chicken quickly absorbs the Jamaican jerk spices, which permeate the meat with their flavor. The delicately scalloped baby pattypan squash benefit from cooking in the microwave, too. Not only do they cook quickly, but they also retain their bright green and yellow colors. To round out the main course, serve boiled rice. A dessert of coffee ice cream or frozen yogurt topped with a warm chocolate sauce enhanced with rum and nutmeg makes a delicious ending to the meal.

Strong flavors abound in this meal, so choose a bountiful wine. Gewürztraminer (dry, best from Alsace) has the complexity and spiciness to pair well here. Alsace producers to look for are Trimbach, Sparr, and Willm.

JERK CHICKEN
The word jerk *refers to the spicing and marinating process comonly used in Caribbean meat cookery.*

   1 small onion, quartered
   1 small clove garlic, halved
   ½ Scotch bonnet chile, or 1 serrano chile, quartered
   3 tablespoons soy sauce
   2 tablespoons wine vinegar
   1 tablespoon light brown sugar
1½ teaspoons cooking oil
   ½ teaspoon ground allspice

¼ teaspoon dried thyme
¼ teaspoon fresh-ground black pepper
⅛ teaspoon ground cloves
⅛ teaspoon ground cinnamon
2 boneless, skinless chicken breasts (about 6 ounces each)

1. Light the grill or heat the broiler. Combine the onion, garlic, and chile in a food processor and pulse until coarsely chopped. Add the soy sauce, vinegar, brown sugar, oil, allspice, thyme, pepper, cloves, and cinnamon and process to a coarse paste.

2. Place the chicken breasts in a microwaveable baking dish with the thinner ends slightly overlapping in the center. Pour the marinade evenly over the chicken, cover, and let stand at room temperature for 10 minutes.

3. Cover the dish with waxed paper and microwave on high, or full, power for 1½ minutes; do not let the marinade boil. Transfer the chicken to a plate and pour the marinade into a microwaveable 2-cup measure.

4. Grill or broil the chicken for 3 to 4 minutes per side, brushing occasionally with the marinade, until lightly charred and just cooked through.

5. To serve, microwave the remaining marinade uncovered on high just until boiling, about 1 minute. Slice the chicken breasts across the grain and arrange on two plates. Serve the warm marinade alongside.

—MARCIA CONE AND THELMA SNYDER

HERBED BABY PATTYPAN SQUASH

To ensure even cooking, arrange the smaller pattypan squash in the center of the casserole and the larger ones around them.

½ pound baby pattypan squash, stems trimmed
1½ teaspoons butter, cut into small bits
½ teaspoon lemon juice
  Salt and fresh-ground black pepper
1 tablespoon minced flat-leaf parsley or chives

GAME PLAN

Light the grill.

Make the jerk sauce and microwave the chicken.

Boil the rice.

Cook the squash.

Grill the chicken.

Make the chocolate sauce shortly before serving dessert.

Arrange the squash in a single layer in a microwaveable casserole. Dot the squash with the butter and sprinkle with the lemon juice and salt and pepper to taste. Cover tightly with microwaveable plastic wrap, turning back one corner slightly. Microwave on high until just tender, about 5 minutes, interrupting the cooking to stir after 3 minutes. Sprinkle the squash with the parsley and serve at once.

—MARCIA CONE AND THELMA SNYDER

JAMAICAN COFFEE SUNDAES

1½ ounces semisweet chocolate chips
1 tablespoon milk
1 tablespoon light corn syrup
Pinch ground nutmeg
1½ teaspoons dark rum
Coffee ice cream or frozen yogurt

In a microwaveable 1-cup measure, combine the chocolate chips, milk, corn syrup, and nutmeg. Microwave uncovered on high until the chocolate mixture melts, about 30 seconds; do not let the chocolate boil. Stir the sauce until smooth and then stir in the rum. Let cool slightly. Spoon the ice cream into bowls and top with the warm sauce.

—MARCIA CONE AND THELMA SNYDER

BLT Update

I t was back in the Fifties that short-order cooks dubbed the bacon, lettuce, and tomato sandwich the BLT. It's a classic combination that deserves a new lease on life. So hold the white bread and mayo. Cook the bacon, marinate the tomato, add arugula and a fresh basil dressing, and you have created a BLT salad. To make it into a substantial main course, top it with garlicky roasted potatoes and crumbled blue cheese and serve it with a good loaf of Italian bread. The quick and easy peach topping is delicious over ice cream and great with angel food or pound cake, too.

Summer is rosé season. Many people have the wrong idea about rosé (candylike, cloying), but a dry southern French one, such as a Tavel—or something a little special, such as a Domaines Ott—will completely change your mind with this meal.

BLT SALAD
The unexpected pungency of blue cheese and garlicky potatoes enhances the basic salad of peppery greens, sweet tomato, and salty bacon.

- 2 tablespoons plus 1 teaspoon olive oil
- 2 teaspoons balsamic vinegar
- 1 tablespoon minced fresh basil,
  plus small whole leaves for garnish
  Salt and fresh-ground black pepper
- 1 medium tomato, cored, seeded, and chopped
- 4 thick slices bacon, cut crosswise into ¾-inch pieces
- 1 large bunch arugula, thick stems removed
  Pan-Roasted Garlic Potatoes (*recipe follows*)
- 2 tablespoons finely chopped Vidalia or other sweet onion
- ¼ cup crumbled blue cheese

1. Combine the oil, vinegar, minced basil, and salt and pepper to taste. Toss 1 tablespoon of the dressing with the tomato. In a frying pan, cook the bacon until crisp. Drain on paper towels.

2. Toss the arugula with the remaining dressing and arrange on two large plates. Scatter the bacon and potatoes over the arugula and sprinkle the onion and blue cheese on top. Scatter the marinated tomato and the basil leaves over the salad and serve.

—JUDITH SUTTON

ABOUT ARUGULA

The spiciness of arugula intensifies as the plant matures; it also varies from bunch to bunch. Be sure to taste a leaf or two before you use this pungent green in salads. Very spicy arugula might require a little extra balsamic vinegar in the dressing to temper the heat, or you can combine the arugula with milder greens, such as baby spinach or *mizuma*.

PAN-ROASTED GARLIC POTATOES

The whole cloves of garlic become sweet and soft after cooking; if you like, remove the garlic skins before serving.

1 tablespoon olive oil
4 large unpeeled cloves garlic
½ pound new potatoes, quartered and
   cut crosswise into ⅜-inch-thick slices
   Salt and fresh-ground black pepper

1. In a large heavy frying pan, heat the oil. Add the garlic and cook over moderate heat, stirring occasionally, until golden, about 5 minutes.

2. Add the potatoes and sprinkle with salt and pepper. Cook, stirring occasionally, until golden brown and tender, about 25 minutes.

—JUDITH SUTTON

GAME PLAN

Make the dressing for the salad.

Marinate the tomato.

Sauté the garlic and potatoes.

Fry the bacon.

Prepare the rest of the salad.

Caramelize the peaches.

ICE CREAM WITH CARAMELIZED PEACHES

It is difficult to improve on a perfect peach except, perhaps, by warming it with a touch of butter and a little brown sugar.

1 tablespoon unsalted butter
2 firm, ripe peaches, peeled and cut into ½-inch-thick slices
2 tablespoons light brown sugar
  Vanilla ice cream

1. In a heavy medium frying pan, melt the butter over moderate heat. Add the peaches, sprinkle with the brown sugar, and stir until it dissolves. Cook, stirring occasionally, until the peaches are tender and the juices are slightly reduced, 5 to 7 minutes longer. Remove the pan from the heat and let cool slightly.

2. Spoon the ice cream into bowls and top with the peaches.

—JUDITH SUTTON

Hot Tuna

As summer settles in, grilling again becomes second nature, and we can tire of the same old burger-or-chicken routine. Then it's time to splurge a little on fresh tuna. For this menu, the meaty fish is topped with a seasoned herb sauce. In place of the usual tossed greens and rice or potatoes, there is a couscous salad studded with carrots and cucumbers. Fresh citrus juices add a refreshing note to the vinaigrette for the salad and to the thirst-quenching drink that goes with the meal. Ice-cream sandwiches—made in a moment with store-bought chocolate wafers—make for a fun dessert.

FRESH LEMON LIMEADE

No frozen concentrate can deliver the sheer delight of fresh-squeezed lemon and lime juices, which are perfect with this dinner.

- ¾ cup sugar
- 3½ cups water
- ½ cup lemon juice
- ½ cup lime juice
- Lemon and lime slices, for serving

In a medium saucepan, combine the sugar and 1 cup of the water. Cook over moderately high heat, stirring to dissolve the sugar. Just before the mixture comes to a boil, remove from the heat. Stir in 2½ cups of cold water and then pour into a pitcher. Stir in the lemon and lime juices and refrigerate. Serve in tall glasses over ice, garnished with lemon and lime slices.

—TRACEY SEAMAN

121

GRILLED TUNA WITH HERBED CREAM

To make two meals at once, cook extra tuna steaks and turn them into a salad for sandwiches (see below).

1 clove garlic, smashed
  Salt
2 tablespoons mayonnaise
3 tablespoons minced fresh chives
2 tablespoons chopped fresh basil
  Fresh-ground black pepper
  Pinch cayenne pepper
2 6-ounce tuna steaks, about ¾ inch thick
2 slices of a large tomato, cut about ⅜ inch thick
¼ cup heavy cream

1. Light the grill or set a heavy grill pan over moderately high heat. On a work surface, using a fork, mash the garlic with ⅛ teaspoon salt. In a small bowl, blend the garlic with the mayonnaise, chives, basil, black pepper to taste, and cayenne.

2. Season the tuna steaks with salt and black pepper and lightly oil the grill or the pan. Grill the tuna for about 3 minutes, then turn the steaks and top each one with a tomato slice. Grill until done to your taste, 2 to 3 minutes for medium rare. Transfer to plates.

3. While the fish is cooking, beat the cream until stiff and fold in the herbed mayonnaise. Serve the fish warm or at room temperature and pass the sauce separately.

—Tracey Seaman

GAME PLAN

Make and freeze the ice-cream sandwiches.

Light the grill.

Make the lemon limeade.

Cook and dress the couscous and then prepare the vegetables for the salad.

Prepare the herbed cream and grill the tuna.

Toss the vegetables with the dressed couscous and serve.

TEMPTING TUNA SALAD

Flake any extra cooked tuna into a bowl. Add finely diced celery, chopped basil, mayonnaise, lemon juice, and salt and pepper. Serve on crusty peasant bread topped with thinly sliced onion and tomato, young greens, and strips of roasted bell pepper. You can also toast the bread, butter it, and rub each side with a garlic clove before making the sandwiches.

GARDEN COUSCOUS SALAD

The salad is also very good with whole wheat couscous.

1½ cups water
   Salt
 1 cup couscous
⅓ cup fresh orange juice
 1 tablespoon white vinegar
 1 teaspoon brown mustard
¼ teaspoon sugar
½ cup olive oil
 1 scallion, including green top, sliced thin
 1 medium carrot, shredded
 1 Kirby cucumber, halved, seeded, and diced
½ jalapeño pepper, seeded and minced
   Fresh-ground black pepper

1. In a medium saucepan, combine the water with a pinch of salt and bring to a boil over moderately high heat. Remove from the heat and stir in the couscous. Cover and let stand for 5 minutes. Fluff the couscous with a fork and transfer to a bowl to cool.

2. In a small glass or stainless-steel bowl, whisk together the orange juice, vinegar, mustard, and sugar. Whisk in the oil. Stir in ½ teaspoon salt. Pour the dressing over the couscous. Add the scallion, carrot, cucumber, and jalapeño and toss well. Season with salt and pepper.

—Tracey Seaman

INSTANT ICE-CREAM SANDWICHES

Make a double batch of these and freeze them for up to three days.

½ cup vanilla ice cream, softened
 8 store-bought crisp chocolate wafer cookies
¼ cup chopped peppermint candies or Heath Bars

Spoon a heaping tablespoon of ice cream onto half of the cookies. Cover with the remaining cookies and press gently. Pat the chopped candies onto the ice cream. Wrap the sandwiches in pairs in waxed paper and freeze until ready to eat.

—Tracey Seaman

PANFRYING SECRET

A spoonful of olive oil and some rosemary sprigs will work magic on a panfried steak. Once the meat has cooked, it takes only a few more seconds to make a flavor-rich oil to drizzle over the top. Just add the rosemary or other seasonings to the frying pan and cook briefly. Sautéed cherry tomatoes, an ear of sweet corn, and good bread complete this satisfying meal. The dessert is foolproof—and it's one of the best ways to present fresh berries of any kind.

Savory steak and the fragrant infused rosemary oil will mingle nicely with a fruity and slightly herbal Chilean merlot—one of the better bargains in the wine bins these days. Also well-priced, and just right for this steak, is a Côtes-du-Rhône red.

STEAK WITH ROSEMARY OIL

The "instant oil" technique works well with many herbs and aromatics. Try substituting hyssop or thyme sprigs or garlic cloves for the rosemary. Or, cook a few sage leaves just until crisp and lightly browned. The fried sage leaves can be used as a garnish.

    2 tablespoons olive oil
¾ to 1 pound well-trimmed boneless sirloin or rib-eye steak,
        cut ¾ inch thick
        Salt and fresh-ground black pepper
    2 3-inch fresh rosemary sprigs, bruised with the back of a
        heavy knife

1. In a large heavy frying pan, heat 1 tablespoon of the oil. When it just begins to smoke, season both sides of the steak

generously with salt and pepper and cook over moderately high heat until done to your taste, 3 minutes per side for medium rare. Transfer the steak to a warmed platter.

2. Add the remaining 1 tablespoon of oil and the rosemary to the pan and stir frequently until the rosemary begins to color, about 1½ minutes. Scrape the oil over the steak, garnish with the rosemary sprigs, and serve.

—JUDITH SUTTON

SAUTÉED CHERRY TOMATOES WITH SHALLOTS

- 2 teaspoons butter
- 2 large shallots, minced
- 1 pint cherry tomatoes, preferably small to medium
  Salt and fresh-ground black pepper

In a large heavy stainless-steel frying pan, melt the butter over moderately high heat. Add the shallots and cherry tomatoes and season with salt and pepper. Cook, stirring occasionally, until the tomatoes start to soften (a few of the skins will split), 3 to 4 minutes. Serve the tomatoes and shallots immediately.

—JUDITH SUTTON

RASPBERRY FOOL

This version of the traditionally smooth puree features crushed berries lightly swirled with whipped cream for more flavor and texture. If you are short on time, simply sprinkle the berries with the sugar, drizzle with the heavy cream, and serve.

- ½ pint raspberries
- 3 to 4 tablespoons sugar, preferably superfine
- 1 cup heavy cream, chilled

In a bowl, using a fork, crush the raspberries with 2 to 3 tablespoons of the sugar. Whip the cream with the remaining 1 tablespoon sugar until firm peaks form. Gently fold in the crushed berries; leave some streaks. Cover the fool and refrigerate until serving time.

—JUDITH SUTTON

GAME PLAN

Make the fool and chill.

Put a pot of water on to boil for the corn.

Husk and cook the corn.

Sauté the steaks and the cherry tomatoes.

SNAPPER FOR SUPPER

An ideal summer supper combines fresh-from-the-garden produce, clean flavors, and dishes that cook in minutes. Here, mild red snapper is coated in cornmeal for a quick panfry. It is served with a creamy tartar sauce (a good commercial one will do in a pinch). On the side, a vegetable salad of green beans, summer squash, bell pepper, and basil, which are all at their peak in July and August. Orzo is perked up with lemon zest and dill, both of which complement the fish beautifully. For dessert, sprinkle fresh blackberries with crème de cassis and serve with a spoonful of heavy cream.

Muscadet de Sèvre-et-Maine is a wonderful match with seafood and ideal for this uncomplicated fish dish. The high acid in the crisp white wine is a great foil for the tartar sauce.

CORNMEAL-TOASTED RED SNAPPER

Have your fishmonger skin the fillets to save time. In place of the snapper, you can substitute any white-fleshed fish, such as sole, haddock, cod, or catfish. The thinner the fillets, the faster they will cook. Serve the fish with your favorite tartar sauce.

¼ cup yellow cornmeal
2 tablespoons flour
½ teaspoon salt
½ teaspoon fresh-ground black pepper
2 skinless red-snapper fillets, about ½- to ¾-inch thick (about 6 ounces each)
2 tablespoons olive oil
   Lime wedges, for serving

1. On a plate, mix together the cornmeal, flour, salt, and pepper. Rinse 1 snapper fillet with cold water, shake off any excess, and dip both sides in the cornmeal mixture to coat. Shake off any excess and transfer the fillet to a clean plate. Repeat with the remaining fillet.

2. In a large heavy frying pan, preferably cast iron, heat the oil over moderately high heat until hot, 3 to 4 minutes. Place the fish fillets in the frying pan and cook, turning once, until the coating is golden brown and the flesh is opaque throughout, 6 to 7 minutes. (Reduce the heat if the fish browns too quickly.)

3. Transfer the fillets to paper towels to drain. Serve with the lime wedges.

—SUSAN SHAPIRO JASLOVE

SUMMER VEGETABLE SALAD

Consider this recipe a template, ready for your own experimentation. If the sugar snap peas look better than the green beans at the farmers' market, by all means buy them. Likewise, baby zucchini can stand in for the summer squash and thin ribbons of radicchio are an alternative for arugula. There is no substitution for fresh basil; its spicy bite is unmatched in the herb garden.

4	ounces green beans, trimmed and halved crosswise
1	small yellow squash, cut into 2-inch pieces
1	small red or green bell pepper, cut into 2-inch pieces
2	tablespoons olive oil
1½	tablespoons balsamic vinegar
	Salt and fresh-ground black pepper
1	small bunch arugula, leaves torn into large pieces
10	large fresh basil leaves, shredded

GAME PLAN

Cook the vegetables for the summer salad.

Boil the orzo.

Fry the fish.

Assemble the salad.

1. In a medium saucepan, bring 1 inch of water to a boil over moderately high heat. Add the beans, cover, and reduce the heat to moderate. Cook until just tender, about 4 minutes. Drain the beans, refresh under cold water, and drain again. Transfer the beans to a serving bowl. Add the squash and bell pepper and toss well.

2. Drizzle the oil over the vegetables and toss to coat evenly. Sprinkle the vinegar on top and toss again. Season with salt and black pepper. Just before serving, add the arugula and basil. Toss and serve.

—SUSAN SHAPIRO JASLOVE

ORZO WITH DILL

¾ cup orzo
1½ teaspoons olive oil
1 teaspoon grated lemon zest
1 tablespoon chopped fresh dill
Salt and fresh-ground black pepper

1. Stir the orzo into a large saucepan of boiling, salted water. Return to a boil and cook until just tender, about 8 minutes. Drain.

2. Return the orzo to the dry saucepan and stir in the oil. Stir in the lemon zest and dill. Season to taste with salt and pepper and serve at once.

—SUSAN SHAPIRO JASLOVE

IT'S SOFT-SHELL CRAB SEASON

Soft-shell crabs, the stars of this meal, are eagerly anticipated at this time of year by their many avid fans. Soft-shells, which are Atlantic blue crabs that have shed their hard shells, are completely edible—claws, body, and all—after cleaning. To guarantee freshness, buy them live from your fishmonger and have them cleaned.

In this menu, a chopped tomato-and-herb sauce does double duty as a coating for the linguine and as an accompaniment to the crabs. Lemon and capers boost the sauce that is served with the crabs, which are quickly sautéed to keep them crisp. An arugula salad with balsamic vinaigrette and Parmesan shavings completes the main course. Sliced fresh apricots with a few Bing cherries, all splashed with some Kirschwasser, make a cheery, refreshing dessert.

The shellfish and the herbaceousnesss of the tomato sauce make for a great pairing with a high-quality pinot grigio. Best bets for an aromatic, flavorful wine are from Collio, in northeast Italy.

SOFT-SHELL CRABS AND LINGUINE
WITH TOMATO HERB SAUCE

If you do not have access to soft-shell crabs, quickly sauté lump crabmeat in butter and spoon it on top of the tomato herb sauce and linguine.

- 1 large tomato, chopped
- 3 tablespoons olive oil
- 1 tablespoon chopped flat-leaf parsley
- 1 tablespoon sliced scallion green
- ½ tablespoon chopped fresh basil
  Salt and fresh-ground black pepper

6 ounces dried linguine
1 tablespoon butter
4 cleaned medium soft-shell crabs
1½ teaspoons lemon juice
1 teaspoon drained capers, chopped
Lemon wedges, for serving

1. In a medium bowl, mix the tomato with 2½ tablespoons of the oil, the parsley, scallion, basil, salt, and pepper. Set the tomato sauce aside at room temperature.

2. Cook the linguine in boiling, salted water, stirring occasionally, until just done, about 10 minutes. Drain and transfer to a large bowl. Add ⅓ cup of the tomato sauce and toss to combine; keep warm.

3. Melt the butter with the remaining ½ tablespoon oil in a large stainless-steel frying pan. Add the crabs and cook over moderately high heat, turning once, until reddish orange and slightly crisp, about 3 minutes per side. Transfer the crabs to a large serving plate and keep warm in a low oven.

4. Add the remaining tomato sauce to the frying pan with the lemon juice and capers and bring to a gentle boil over moderate heat. Cook until the tomatoes have just softened and the sauce is slightly reduced, about 1 minute. Season with salt and pepper.

5. Divide the linguine between two large plates. Spoon the tomato-caper sauce on top of the pasta. Set two soft-shell crabs on each mound of linguine and serve with lemon wedges.

—STEPHANIE LYNESS

GAME PLAN

Put a large pot of water on to boil for the pasta.

Make the tomato herb sauce.

Wash the arugula and make the dressing.

Cook the pasta.

Sauté the crabs and finish their sauce.

Toss the salad.

KEEPING LEAFY HERBS FRESH

Wash and spin-dry flat-leaf parsley or basil and then trim the stem ends. Put them in a tall container and add enough water to submerge the stems. Store parsley in the refrigerator, but keep basil at room temperature or the leaves will turn black. These herbs will keep for several days.

ARUGULA, BASIL, AND PARMESAN SALAD
Use a vegetable peeler to carve cheese curls from a chunk of Parmesan.

- 1 tablespoon balsamic vinegar
  Salt and fresh-ground black pepper
- 1 tablespoon plus 1 teaspoon olive oil
- 1 small bunch arugula (about 4 ounces), stems removed
- 6 large fresh basil leaves, cut into thin slices
- 1 ounce Parmesan shavings

In a large salad bowl, whisk the vinegar with salt and pepper to taste. Whisk in the oil. Add the arugula and basil and toss to combine. Spoon the salad onto plates and scatter the Parmesan shavings on top.

—STEPHANIE LYNESS

MEXICAN GRILLED PORK

P reparing authentic Mexican food often requires a search for hard-to-find ingredients. This menu is an exception. The intensely flavored chile sauce that tops the pork steaks is made in the blender with only five supermarket items: ancho chiles, pineapple juice, cider vinegar, garlic, and cooking oil. The pork, vegetables, and bananas can all be cooked outdoors on the grill or inside in the oven.

Smooth, flavorful Rioja Reserva (or even the more expensive Gran Reserva) will stand up to the robust ancho sauce and will not be too overbearing for the delicacy of the pork. Alternatively, try a fruity California chardonnay.

PORK STEAKS WITH ANCHO SAUCE
Serve any extra ancho sauce the next day with scrambled eggs and fried tortillas for a different take on the Mexican dish huevos rancheros. *Or put it on chicken, hamburgers, even hot dogs.*

- 2 large dried ancho chiles
- ½ cup boiling water
- 2 tablespoons cider vinegar
- 2 tablespoons plus 2 teaspoons cooking oil
- ½ cup pineapple juice
- 2 large cloves garlic
  Salt and fresh-ground black pepper
- 2 boneless pork loin steaks (about 6 ounces each), trimmed of fat
- 2 tablespoons minced red onion

1. In a medium frying pan, toast the anchos over high heat, turning and pressing down on them with a metal spatula to flatten, until pliable, about 1 minute. Remove the seeds and veins from the chiles and rinse well. Transfer to a medium bowl, add the boiling water and vinegar, and let soak, keeping the chiles submerged, until softened, about 20 minutes.

2. Light the grill or heat the broiler. Heat the 2 tablespoons of oil in a medium stainless-steel saucepan. In a blender, puree the anchos and their soaking liquid with the pineapple juice, garlic, and ½ teaspoon salt. Pass the sauce through a coarse strainer into the hot oil and cook over high heat, stirring constantly, until slightly thickened, about 7 minutes. Season with salt and pepper.

3. Rub the pork steaks with the remaining 2 teaspoons of oil and season with salt and pepper. Grill or broil the steaks for about 4 minutes per side, turning once, until just cooked through. Let rest a few minutes, ladle half of the ancho sauce over the steaks, and slice. Serve sprinkled with the red onion. Pass the additional sauce.

—CHATA DuBOSE

GAME PLAN

Toast and soak the anchos. Meanwhile, parboil and marinate the vegetables.

Light the grill.

Make the ancho sauce.

Warm the tortillas.

Season the pork and grill or broil with the vegetables.

Just before dessert, make the sweetened cream and grill the bananas.

LIME-GRILLED VEGETABLES

2 medium potatoes, cut into ½-inch-thick slices
2 carrots, cut on the diagonal into ¼-inch-thick slices
¼ cup olive oil
1 tablespoon lime juice
1 tablespoon grated onion
¼ teaspoon ground cumin
¼ teaspoon salt
  Fresh-ground black pepper
1 large zucchini, cut on the diagonal into ¾-inch-thick slices

1. Bring a medium saucepan of water to a boil. Add the potatoes and carrots and parboil over high heat for 10 minutes. Drain and set aside.

2. Light the grill or heat the broiler. In a large bowl, combine the oil, lime juice, onion, cumin, salt, and pepper to taste. Add the

potatoes, carrots, and zucchini and toss to coat. Let the vegetables stand for up to 15 minutes.

3. Grill or broil the sliced vegetables for about 3 minutes per side, turning once, until nicely browned and tender. Serve hot.

—CHATA DUBOSE

GRILLED BANANAS WITH SWEETENED CREAM

If you like, use whipped heavy cream instead of sour cream as a topping for the grilled bananas.

½ cup sour cream
¼ teaspoon vanilla extract
1 teaspoon light brown sugar
1 large firm banana, cut on the diagonal
  into ½-inch-thick slices
1 tablespoon unsalted butter, melted
¼ teaspoon cinnamon

1. Light the grill, if using. In a small bowl, stir together the sour cream, vanilla, and brown sugar until the sugar is dissolved.

2. In a medium bowl, sprinkle the banana slices with the melted butter and cinnamon. Grill the bananas or panfry in a large non-stick frying pan over moderately high heat, turning, until golden, about 2 minutes per side. Transfer the bananas to individual plates and spoon the sweetened cream on top.

—CHATA DUBOSE

ZESTY LOBSTER WITH LIME

Lobster can be cooked in many ways—grilled, sautéed, sauced, bisqued—but steaming is the easiest for the weeknight cook. Theoretically, you should use a lobster pot with a steamer rack, but a steamer basket works just as well. Here, the classic drawn butter accompaniment is modified by adding a splash of lime juice. The green salad with mango complements the lobsters' flavors and meaty texture. The blueberry shortcake is made with cake flour, a sure method that produces a very tender biscuit.

Lobster and drawn butter is a classic match with the power and steeliness of a great bottle of Chablis. If riper flavors are more your style, a California sauvignon blanc will give the desired fullness without sacrificing palate-refreshing acidity.

STEAMED LOBSTER WITH LIME BUTTER
These lobsters are served whole, so be sure to supply lobster crackers with which to tackle the meal.

> 2 live lobsters (about 1½ pounds each)
> 4 tablespoons butter
> 2 tablespoons lime juice (1 lime)
> Lime wedges, for serving

1. In a large pot with a steamer basket, bring 2 inches of salted water to a boil over high heat. Add the lobsters, cover, and steam until they turn bright orange, about 12 minutes.

2. Meanwhile, in a small saucepan, melt the butter over moderate heat. Remove from the heat and stir in the lime juice. Pour the

lime butter into 2 small ramekins or bowls. Serve each person a lobster with lime wedges and a ramekin of lime butter.

—STEPHANIE LYNESS

GREEN SALAD WITH MANGO AND A CITRUS VINAIGRETTE

2 tablespoons fresh orange juice
1 teaspoon wine vinegar
1 teaspoon lemon juice
   Salt and fresh-ground black pepper
3 tablespoons olive oil
1 ripe small mango
1 head Boston or red-leaf lettuce, torn into 2-inch pieces

1. In a salad bowl, combine the orange juice, vinegar, and lemon juice. Season with salt and pepper to taste. Gradually whisk in the oil until blended.

2. With a small sharp knife, peel the mango. Place the mango on a flat surface and cut in half just above the pit. Turn and repeat on the other side. Cut away any remaining flesh and cut into ½-inch dice. Just before serving, add the lettuce and mango to the salad bowl; toss to coat with the vinaigrette and serve.

—STEPHANIE LYNESS

BLUEBERRY SHORTCAKE

This recipe makes four biscuits; wrap and freeze two of them for next week's shortcake.

½ cup all-purpose flour
½ cup cake flour
1½ teaspoons baking powder
¼ teaspoon salt
3 tablespoons plus 1 teaspoon sugar
4 tablespoons cold butter, cut into small pieces
1 cup heavy cream
¼ teaspoon cinnamon

GAME PLAN

Heat the oven.

Bake the shortcake.

Prepare the greens, mango, and vinaigrette.

Toss the blueberries with sugar and lemon juice.

Steam the lobsters.

Toss the salad.

1½ cups fresh blueberries
1 teaspoon lemon juice

1. Heat the oven to 450°. In a food processor, combine the all-purpose and cake flours, the baking powder, salt, and 1 tablespoon of the sugar; process until blended. Add the butter and process until the mixture resembles coarse meal. Add ⅓ cup plus 1 tablespoon of the cream and process just until a dough forms, 1 to 2 seconds.

2. Turn the dough out on a lightly floured work surface and knead a few times. Form the dough into a ball and place it on an ungreased cookie sheet. Pat the dough out to form a ¾-inch-thick round. Cut the round into quarters and arrange them about 1 inch apart. In a small bowl, combine the cinnamon and the 1 teaspoon of sugar. Sprinkle the top of the dough with the cinnamon sugar. Bake until very lightly browned, about 12 minutes. Let cool for 5 minutes.

3. Meanwhile, in a medium bowl, toss the blueberries with the lemon juice and the remaining 2 tablespoons sugar; crush some of the berries and set aside. In a medium bowl, whip the remaining (scant ⅔ cup) cream until firm peaks form.

4. Split two biscuits in half and put the bottom halves on two plates. Spoon half of the blueberry mixture over each biscuit, cover with the other biscuit half, and spoon the whipped cream on top.

—STEPHANIE LYNESS

SEAFOOD LOVERS' SALAD

C hilled seafood has a delicate, almost sweet, clean flavor that is highlighted by simple seasonings but can be masked by sharper accents such as garlic or strong herbs and spices. A salad that combines three favorite seafoods is a summer-time delight.

The stove time for this meal is minimal. If you can buy cooked shrimp from a top-notch fishmonger, you need only cook the squid, which is available already cleaned. If you steam, poach, or boil the shrimp yourself, tag on a little extra time. Serve the seafood salad with sliced fresh tomatoes, sourdough bread, and a cooling drink of citrus-flavored iced tea. For an easy, delicious dessert, fresh ricotta cheese is sweetened and sieved to give it the feel of a mild, creamy pudding. Top it with berries and, if you like, some grated chocolate.

ORANGE ICED TEA

Vary this drink by adding a splash of sparkling water or fruit juice, such as cranberry or pineapple. The recipe makes one quart.

- 3 black tea bags
- 1 cup boiling water
- 1 cup cold water
- 2 cups fresh orange juice (from about 5 oranges)
  - Ice
  - Lemon slices
  - Sugar (optional)

1. In a large glass measuring cup, brew the tea in the boiling water for 5 minutes. Gently squeeze the tea bags; discard.

141

2. In a pitcher, combine the brewed tea, cold water, and orange juice. Serve in tall glasses over ice with a slice of lemon. Sweeten with sugar to taste.

—STEPHANIE LYNESS

SEAFOOD SALAD

Select a light yet fruity extra-virgin olive oil to complement the clean seafood flavors in this salad.

- 6 ounces cleaned squid, bodies cut into ¼-inch rings, tentacles halved if large
- 6 ounces shelled, cooked medium shrimp
- 4 ounces lump crabmeat, picked over
- 1 small red bell pepper, quartered lengthwise and cut crosswise into ¼-inch-thick strips
- 1 scallion, including green top, sliced
- ¼ cup chopped celery
- 1 tablespoon chopped fresh basil
- 2 tablespoons lemon juice
  Salt and fresh-ground black pepper
- ¼ cup olive oil
- 4 radicchio leaves

1. In a medium saucepan, bring 2 inches of water to a boil over moderately high heat. Stir in the squid, cover, and cook until just tender, 2 to 3 minutes. Drain and rinse under cold running water; drain thoroughly. Transfer to a large bowl and add the shrimp, crabmeat, bell pepper, scallion, celery, and basil. Toss well.

2. Whisk the lemon juice with salt and black pepper to taste. Whisk in the oil. Pour over the salad and toss gently.

3. Place 2 radicchio leaves on each plate or line a small platter with the leaves; mound the salad on top.

—STEPHANIE LYNESS

GAME PLAN

Brew the tea and refrigerate.

Cook the squid and assemble the salad.

Prepare the dessert.

FRESH BERRIES WITH RICOTTA CHEESE

Make sure you choose a creamy whole-milk ricotta. Choosing a part-skim ricotta will give the dessert an unwanted graininess.

½ pound fresh ricotta
1 tablespoon grated orange zest (from 1 orange)
1 tablespoon sugar
1 cup mixed berries, such as raspberries, blueberries, blackberries, and strawberries
1½ tablespoons fresh orange juice
Grated bittersweet chocolate (optional)

1. Press the ricotta through a strainer set over a bowl. Stir in the orange zest and sugar. Spoon the ricotta onto two dessert plates.

2. Toss the berries with the orange juice and chocolate to taste. Spoon the berries over the ricotta.

—STEPHANIE LYNESS

SWEET CORN AND PASTA

There is a brief period in the summer during which the tomatoes are at their ripest and the corn is at its sweetest, and it's so hot that the last thing you want to do is to cook dinner. Here is the perfect meal for nights like these. The fresh tomato sauce for the pasta is not cooked, but merely warmed over the boiling pasta water. A simple salad and a slice or two of Italian bread are the only accompaniments you will need. Dessert is pure refreshment—a cooling watermelon and strawberry puree.

Seek out an Alsace pinot blanc or even an Italian pinot bianco to match the luscious character of the pappardelle, but beware too much heat in the sauce or it will overwhelm any wine. In which case, try iced tea, lemonade, or beer.

NEW WORLD PAPPARDELLE

Be careful when handling the lantern-shaped habañero—it is probably the hottest pepper you can buy. For more timid palates, substitute a serrano or jalapeño.

- 2 large ears of corn, shucked
- 1½ pounds ripe tomatoes, cored and cut into ½- to 1-inch dice
- ¼ cup olive oil
- ¼ cup chopped fresh cilantro
- ¼ to ½ habañero chile, seeded and minced
- 1 teaspoon coarse salt
- ½ pound dried pappardelle or other wide noodles

1. In a large saucepan of boiling, salted water, cook the corn until barely tender, about 2 minutes. Remove and let cool slightly

and then cut the kernels from the cobs with a sharp knife. In a large stainless-steel bowl, toss the corn with the tomatoes, oil, cilantro, habañero, and salt.

2. In a large pot of boiling, salted water, cook the pappardelle until just done, about 12 minutes.

3. While the pappardelle cooks, carefully hold the metal bowl over the boiling water, shaking it occasionally, until the tomatoes are just warmed through. Drain the pappardelle and add it to the bowl. Toss well and serve immediately.

—JOHANNE KILLEEN AND GEORGE GERMON

PASTA POINTERS

Make sure you use ample water to cook pasta—six quarts for one pound of pasta. Cover the pot so the water comes to a boil quickly.

Salt the water just before adding the pasta; use three and a half tablespoons of coarse salt for six quarts of water. Water that tastes slightly salty will enhance the flavor of the pasta.

Reserve some of the pasta-cooking water before you drain the pasta. If a sauce is too thick, a little pasta-cooking water will lighten it; if a sauce is too thin, add pasta-cooking water and then reduce it. The starch will thicken the sauce.

MIXED GREENS WITH CREAMY PARMESAN-AND-PINE-NUT DRESSING

 2 tablespoons grated Parmesan
 2 tablespoons fresh basil leaves
 1 tablespoon toasted pine nuts
 ½ teaspoon minced garlic
 ⅓ cup olive oil
2½ tablespoons balsamic vinegar
4 to 5 cups mixed salad greens

GAME PLAN

Put a pot of water on to boil for the pappardelle.

Prepare the fruit cup.

Blend the salad dressing.

Boil the pappardelle; prepare the sauce.

1. In a food processor or blender, puree the Parmesan, basil, pine nuts, and garlic. Slowly add the oil, processing continuously. Add the vinegar and pulse to combine.

2. In a salad bowl, toss half of the dressing with the greens. (*Cover the remaining dressing and store in the refrigerator for later use.*)

—CHRIS SCHLESINGER AND JOHN WILLOUGHBY

STRAWBERRY-AND-WATERMELON CUP

1 ¼-pound wedge of watermelon, rind and seeds discarded, cut into chunks (about 2 cups)
½ pint strawberries
1½ teaspoons sugar
2 fresh mint sprigs, for garnish

In a food processor, process the watermelon, strawberries, and sugar until smooth. Pass the mixture through a strainer into a bowl, pressing with a rubber spatula. Rinse the strainer and strain the mixture again. Pour into two stemmed glasses. Chill. Serve with a mint sprig on top.

—DIANA STURGIS

SALAD STYLE

"Salads afford considerable scope for the exercise of individual taste," opined Isabella Beeton, the British author of *Mrs. Beeton's Book of Household Management*. Her words, now more than one-and-a-half centuries old, still ring true today. There are few rules for the creation of a salad except that the greens be fresh and crisp. While we can be almost certain she never sat down to a salad like the one presented here—frisée, goat cheese, bacon, beans, and croutons—we think she would have agreed that this is the perfect meal for a hot summer's evening. The meal begins with a tapenade with a twist—mint and red-pepper flakes add freshness and heat. Serve it with toasted rounds of French bread called crostini. The dessert of peaches in wine and honey will both refresh and delight.

New Zealand sauvignon blanc is the usual choice with goat cheese, but the bacon in the dressing, along the zesty tapenade, requires a little more weight. Sauvignon blanc from warmer California has fuller fruit, with the acidic backbone lingering in the background.

OLIVE CAPER TAPENADE WITH FRESH MINT
You can make this slightly spicy tapenade with both oil-cured and brine-cured olives; just be sure to use large ones, which are easier to pit. This recipe makes about two thirds of a cup of tapenade; refrigerate the leftover tapenade and serve it with grilled steak or chicken.

½ cup flat-leaf parsley leaves
¼ cup fresh mint leaves
¼ cup olive oil

2 tablespoon capers, drained
⅛ teaspoon dried red-pepper flakes
1 cup assorted olives (about 5 ounces), pitted

In a food processor, pulse the parsley, mint, oil, capers, and red-pepper flakes until finely chopped. Add the olives and pulse until finely chopped but not pureed. (*The tapenade can be refrigerated for up to 3 days. Let return to room temperature before serving.*)

—GRACE PARISI

FRISÉE SALAD WITH BEANS AND WARM BACON DRESSING

This salad offers many contrasting flavors and textures: tangy goat cheese and slightly bitter frisée; creamy beans, juicy tomatoes, and crisp croutons—all tossed with a warm bacon dressing. The tender white leaves from the center of a head of chicory or escarole are a good substitute for the frisée.

1 cup cubed crustless peasant bread (¾-inch cubes)
1 tablespoon plus 1 teaspoon olive oil
3 strips thick-sliced bacon, cut crosswise in ¾-inch pieces
1 shallot, sliced thin
1½ tablespoons Champagne vinegar or white-wine vinegar
Salt and fresh-ground black pepper
4 ounces frisée, torn into 2-inch pieces
¾ cup cooked navy beans, rinsed if canned
Several yellow or red cherry tomatoes, halved
2 ounces mild goat cheese, crumbled

GAME PLAN

Macerate the peaches.

Heat the oven.

Make the tapenade; toast the crostini.

Prepare the salad.

1. Heat the oven to 350°. Toss the bread cubes with the 1 teaspoon of oil and arrange in a single layer in a baking dish. Bake for about 8 minutes, or until golden but not dry.

2. In a medium stainless-steel frying pan, fry the bacon over moderately high heat until crisp. Transfer the bacon to paper towels to drain. Add the remaining 1 tablespoon oil to the fat in the pan. Add the shallot and cook over moderate heat, stirring occasionally, until just beginning to brown, about 7 minutes. Stir in the vinegar, season with salt and pepper, and keep warm.

3. In a large bowl, toss the frisée with the beans, bacon, toasted croutons, and tomatoes. Add the dressing and toss. Add the goat cheese and toss gently but thoroughly. Serve immediately.

—GRACE PARISI

PEACHES IN MUSCAT WITH HONEY

Use your hand to crush the basil leaves lightly and release their fragrance into this elegant dessert.

⅓ cup dessert wine, such as Beaumes-de-Venise or
    California Muscat
⅓ cup crushed fresh basil leaves
 1 tablespoon plus 1 teaspoon honey
 2 large ripe peaches, preferably white, cut into thin slices

In a glass bowl, combine the wine, basil, and honey. Add the peaches and let stand at room temperature for 30 minutes. Refrigerate for up to 4 hours before serving.

—MARCIA KIESEL

Fall

Cheddar-Cheese Polenta with Mushroom Ragout (p. 173)

Teriyaki Chicken (p. 183) and Noodles with Spicy Peanut Sauce (p.184)

FAST MOROCCAN FEAST

A large helping of saucy vegetables over a mound of steaming couscous is a soothing, delicious end to a chilly autumn day. Tonight's vegetarian feast is Moroccan in inspiration, a savory mingling of sweet pepper, tomatoes, potatoes, carrots, and chickpeas infused with saffron, cumin, and cinnamon. If you desire a salad, sprinkle sliced oranges with a little diced red onion. For dessert, serve fresh dates with almond cookies, which are made here without flour. Sweetened mint tea is the traditional Moroccan beverage.

MOROCCAN VEGETABLE STEW

Harissa—a condiment made from hot peppers, garlic, and spices—can be stirred into the stew just before serving to increase the level of heat.

1 tablespoon cooking oil
1 small onion, sliced thin
1 small red bell pepper, sliced
½ teaspoon cinnamon
1 teaspoon ground cumin
⅛ to ¼ teaspoon dried red-pepper flakes
2 canned plum tomatoes with ¼ cup of their juice
1 tablespoon lime juice
⅛ teaspoon saffron threads
½ cup diced new potatoes
½ cup diced carrots
¼ cup water
1 cup cooked chickpeas, rinsed if canned
½ teaspoon salt
  Harissa (optional)

1. In a Dutch oven, heat the oil over moderate heat. Add the onion, bell pepper, cinnamon, cumin, and red-pepper flakes and cook, stirring occasionally, until the vegetables are soft, about 5 minutes.

2. Add the tomatoes with their juice; breaking them up with a large spoon. Add the lime juice, saffron, potatoes, carrots, and water and bring to a boil. Cover, reduce the heat to moderately low, and simmer, stirring occasionally, until the potatoes and carrots are tender, about 20 minutes.

3. Stir in the chickpeas; cover and simmer until the chickpeas are warmed through, about 5 minutes. Season with the salt and the harissa, if using.

—SUSAN SHAPIRO JASLOVE

WHOLE-WHEAT COUSCOUS

Whole-wheat couscous, which is available in health-food stores, has a wonderful nutty flavor, but feel free to use the more traditional refined product and follow the package directions.

1½ cups water
 2 tablespoons butter
½ teaspoon salt
 1 cup couscous, preferably whole wheat

In a medium saucepan, combine the water with the butter and salt and bring to a boil over high heat. Stir in the couscous. Reduce the heat to low, cover, and cook for 5 minutes. Fluff the couscous with a fork before serving.

—SUSAN SHAPIRO JASLOVE

GAME PLAN

Heat the oven.

Bake the cookies.

Make the stew.

Prepare the couscous.

Brew the mint tea.

ALMOND OAT COOKIES

Pack leftover cookies in a small tin; they will keep for a week.

½ cup whole almonds, plus 12 for garnish
½ cup old-fashioned rolled oats
⅛ teaspoon salt
¼ cup dark brown sugar

  2 tablespoons cold butter, cut into bits
2 to 3 drops almond extract
  1 tablespoon water

1. Heat the oven to 350°. Lightly grease a large baking sheet. In a food processor, combine the ½ cup almonds with the oats, salt, and brown sugar; process until finely ground and mealy. Add the butter, almond extract, and water. Process until the dough just forms a ball.

2. Divide the dough into 12 equal portions. Form each into a ball and place on the prepared baking sheet. Flatten the balls into circles about ¼ inch thick. Press a whole almond into the top of each cookie. Bake for 13 minutes, or until the cookies are set and barely browned around the edges. Do not overbake. Let cool on the baking sheet before serving.

—SUSAN SHAPIRO JASLOVE

A PEPPY SCALLOP CHOWDER

When the days grow shorter, a hearty chowder is one of the most comforting dishes you can put on the dinner table. This one's main ingredients—scallops, potatoes, leeks, and cream—combine to create a creamy texture and a balanced flavor. Red bell pepper adds visual liveliness, and a jalapeño pepper lends a subtle heat to the broth. Follow the chowder with a salad of mixed greens, dressed with a simple vinaigrette. Finish the meal with crisp chocolate cookies and espresso.

Verdicchio dei Castelli di Jesi (or the rarer Verdicchio di Matelica) would be a minerally, herbaceous counterpoint to the flavorful chowder. The balanced acidity of either of these wines from the center of Italy will keep the palate fresh as well.

SCALLOP-AND-POTATO CHOWDER WITH LEEKS

For a milder chowder, seed the jalapeño before mincing it.

½ pound small new potatoes
1½ teaspoons butter
2 small leeks, white and tender green parts, sliced crosswise
1 medium red bell pepper, cut into 1-inch pieces
1 medium jalapeño pepper, minced
¾ cup chicken stock or canned low-sodium chicken broth
½ cup bottled clam juice
¼ teaspoon dried thyme, crumbled
Salt and fresh-ground black pepper
½ pound large sea scallops, halved crosswise
¼ cup light cream
2 tablespoons minced flat-leaf parsley

1. In a steamer basket set over 3 inches of boiling water, steam the potatoes until tender, about 15 minutes.

2. Melt the butter in a medium saucepan. Add the leeks, bell pepper, and jalapeño. Cover and cook over moderate heat, stirring occasionally, until softened, about 10 minutes.

3. Quarter the steamed potatoes. Add the stock and clam juice to the casserole and bring to a simmer over moderate heat. Stir in the potatoes and thyme and season with salt and black pepper.

4. Add the scallops and cream to the hot stew. Simmer gently, stirring occasionally, until the scallops are just cooked through, about 4 minutes. Stir in the parsley, season with salt and black pepper, and serve at once.

—ANN CLARK

VARIATION: SHRIMP-AND-POTATO CHOWDER
The slightly spicy chowder base also works well with shrimp: Buy ¾ pound medium shrimp in their shells (1 pound if the shrimp are whole). Clean the shrimp and put the shells and heads, if available, in a large stainless-steel saucepan. Add water to cover, plus 2 tablespoons white wine, some chopped onion and celery, parsley, a few peppercorns, and a bay leaf. Bring to a boil over moderate heat and simmer for 30 minutes. Strain the stock into a smaller saucepan and boil until it is reduced to ¾ cup. Use this fragrant shrimp stock to replace the chicken stock in the above recipe. Proceed with the recipe as directed above, simmering the peeled shrimp in the hot chowder until cooked through, about 3 minutes.

CHOCOLATE CRISPS

¼ pound unsalted butter
3 ounces semisweet chocolate, chopped
¾ cup sugar
1 large egg, beaten
1 teaspoon vanilla extract
1½ cups flour
½ teaspoon baking soda
Pinch salt

GAME PLAN

Heat the oven.

Put a pot of water on to boil for steaming the potatoes.

Make the cookies.

Prepare the chowder up to the point of adding the scallops.

Wash the lettuce and make a vinaigrette and assemble the salad.

Finish the chowder.

1. Heat the oven to 375°. In a heavy medium saucepan, melt the butter and chocolate over low heat, stirring constantly, until smooth. Remove from the heat. Alternatively, melt the butter and chocolate in a microwave oven on high, or full, power for 2 minutes. Stir until smooth.

2. Stir ½ cup of the sugar into the chocolate. Stir in the egg and vanilla. Add the flour, baking soda, and salt and stir until blended.

3. Drop tablespoons of the dough about 2 inches apart onto two large baking sheets. Spread the remaining ¼ cup sugar on a small plate. Oil the bottom of a glass and dip it into the sugar and then press down on a cookie to flatten slightly; the sugar will keep the glass from sticking. Repeat with the remaining cookies.

4. Bake the cookies on the upper and lower racks of the oven for about 15 minutes, switching the pans halfway through cooking, until the edges are crisp. Transfer to a rack to cool. (*The cookies can be kept for up to three days in an airtight container.*)

—ANN CLARK

LEMONY LAMB CHOPS

L amb chops are ideal for fast dinners because they cook quickly and are best when served simply. For these broiled chops, which are marinated briefly in oil redolent of lemon, thyme, and pepper, you can use either loin or rib chops. Accompany the lamb with a crusty potato pancake and carrots, which glaze as they cook in their sweet, buttery braising liquid. For a seasonal finale, serve fresh pears for dessert.

Lamb's slightly gamy edge and full flavor is best matched with a deep, robust red—usually cabernet sauvignon. A fine Bordeaux is a classic pairing, as would be a Bordeaux-style Meritage blend from California.

LEMON PEPPER LAMB CHOPS

To save time, begin marinating the lamb chops in the lemon pepper oil in the morning; keep them in the refrigerator.

- 1 teaspoon grated lemon zest
- 1 teaspoon cracked black pepper
- 1 teaspoon fresh thyme
- ¼ teaspoon salt
- 1 tablespoon olive oil
- 4 lamb loin chops, cut 1 inch thick and trimmed of excess fat

1. In a small bowl, combine the lemon zest, pepper, thyme, and salt. Stir in the oil. Rub the lamb chops on both sides with the lemon pepper marinade and transfer to a plate. Let stand at room temperature for at least 30 minutes.

2. Heat the broiler. Set the lamb chops on a broiler pan. Broil, turning once and brushing with any remaining marinade, until the lamb chops are done to taste, about 6 minutes per side for medium rare. Let rest for 5 minutes and then transfer to plates and serve.

—SUSAN SHAPIRO JASLOVE

BIG POTATO PANCAKE

1 pound medium all-purpose potatoes, peeled
1 small onion
½ teaspoon salt
⅛ teaspoon fresh-ground black pepper
2 tablespoons olive oil

1. In a medium saucepan, cover the potatoes with water. Cover the pan and bring to a boil over moderately high heat. Uncover and parboil the potatoes for 5 minutes.

2. Drain the potatoes and rinse with cold water. Shred the potatoes and the onion in a food processor fitted with a shredding disk or grate on a box grater. Transfer the potato mixture to a bowl and toss with the salt and pepper.

3. Heat 1 tablespoon of the oil in a 10-inch nonstick frying pan. Spread the potato mixture evenly in the pan, patting it down with a spatula. Cook the potato pancake over moderately high heat until it is deep golden brown on the bottom, about 10 minutes.

4. Hold a baking sheet or a large platter directly over the pan and, using pot holders, carefully invert the potato pancake onto it. Heat the remaining 1 tablespoon oil in the pan. Slide the pancake back into the pan, uncooked-side down, and cook until the bottom is nicely browned, about 10 minutes more. Slide the potato pancake onto a cutting board, cut it into 4 wedges, and serve immediately.

—SUSAN SHAPIRO JASLOVE

GAME PLAN

Prepare the lemon pepper oil and marinate the lamb chops.

Meanwhile, peel and boil the potatoes.

Cut the carrots and start them cooking.

Shred the potatoes and begin to brown them.

Broil the lamb while the potato pancake finishes cooking.

GLAZED CARROTS

Buy packaged peeled baby carrots, available in many supermarkets, to save the time spent peeling and cutting regular carrots.

¾ pound thin carrots, peeled and cut into 1-inch lengths
2 teaspoons butter
1 teaspoon dark or light brown sugar
¼ teaspoon salt
¼ teaspoon grated nutmeg
  Pinch cinnamon
⅔ cup water
  Fresh-ground black pepper

Put the carrots in a medium saucepan. Add the butter, brown sugar, salt, nutmeg, cinnamon, and water. Bring to a boil over high heat. Lower the heat to moderate and simmer, shaking the pan occasionally, until the carrots are tender and lightly glazed, 15 to 20 minutes. If necessary, continue cooking the carrots over moderately high heat to evaporate any remaining liquid. Season the glazed carrots with pepper.

—SUSAN SHAPIRO JASLOVE

A ONE-POT WONDER

Casseroles have pretty much gone the way of LPs and harvest-gold appliances, but a meal whose ingredients cook together in a single pot still has much appeal. This thoroughly modern one-dish dinner combines an assortment of roasted vegetables with cream, two cheeses, parsley, and fusilli and bakes until bubbling and browned. Garlic bread is all you need to finish out the main course. For dessert there is warm and luscious peach crisp served with vanilla ice cream.

This is an easy dish to match with a medium- to light-bodied white—sauvignon blanc or pinot grigio. For an unusual one, look for an Arneis, Piedmont's most interesting white variety. The wine is crisp with nutty accents and a good finish.

BAKED FUSILLI WITH ROASTED VEGETABLES

To save cooking time, cut the vegetables into small pieces. The pasta can be assembled in advance and refrigerated until baking time. Remove the dish from the refrigerator when you turn the oven on and increase the baking time as necessary.

1 medium red onion, halved and cut into ¼-inch-thick slices
2 medium carrots, halved lengthwise and cut crosswise into ¼-inch-thick slices
1 small zucchini, quartered lengthwise and cut crosswise into ¼-inch-thick rounds
1 small red bell pepper, cut into ¼-inch dice
1 tablespoon olive oil
1 clove garlic, minced
½ pound fusilli

1 cup heavy cream
⅓ cup canned chopped tomatoes in puree
1 tablespoon minced flat-leaf parsley
3 ounces fontina, shredded (about ¾ cup)
¼ cup grated Parmesan
    Salt and fresh-ground black pepper

1. Heat the oven to 450°. Toss the onion, carrots, zucchini, and bell pepper with the oil and spread on a large baking sheet. Roast for 20 to 25 minutes, stirring several times, until caramelized and golden brown. Transfer to a bowl, add the garlic, and toss well. Reduce the oven temperature to 425°.

2. Meanwhile, cook the fusilli in boiling, salted water, stirring occasionally, until just done, about 11 minutes. Drain.

3. Add the pasta to the roasted vegetables along with the cream, tomatoes, parsley, fontina, and 2 tablespoons of the Parmesan. Season with salt and pepper; stir well. Transfer to an 8-inch-square baking pan; top with the remaining 2 tablespoons Parmesan. Bake for 15 to 20 minutes, or until bubbling and golden brown. Let the pasta rest for 5 minutes before serving.

—JUDITH SUTTON

MELTINGLY GOOD FONTINA

Delectable and very creamy, fontina is produced on the alpine slopes of northern Italy, in the Val d'Aosta. The large wheels of handcrafted cheese are made from full-fat cow's milk, and the cheese is said to taste faintly of wildflowers and herbs. Fontina is a superb cheese for melting, and it is used in the Italian version of fondue called *fonduta*. Fontinas are also made in Denmark, France, and the United States, but they often lack the depth or firm texture of a true Fontina Val d'Aosta.

GAME PLAN

Heat the oven to 450°.

Put a large pot of water on to boil for the pasta.

Roast the vegetables; when done, reduce oven temperature to 425°.

Cook the fusilli.

Toss the pasta with the roasted vegetables and cheese and bake.

Assemble the peach crisp.

Reduce the oven temperature to 375°; then bake the crisps while you dine.

WARM PEACH CRISP

1 pound frozen sliced peaches, thawed
⅓ cup flour
¼ cup light brown sugar
¼ teaspoon cinnamon
2 tablespoons cold unsalted butter, cut into small pieces
    Vanilla ice cream, for serving

1. Heat the oven to 375°. Generously butter two individual baking dishes; they should be about 6 inches wide and 1 inch deep. Divide the peaches between the two dishes.

2. In a small bowl, toss together the flour, brown sugar, and cinnamon. Work in the butter with your fingertips until the mixture resembles coarse meal. Scatter evenly over the peaches. Bake for 20 minutes, or until the top is lightly browned and bubbly. Serve with the vanilla ice cream.

—ANNE WALSH

SALMON STARS

Salmon is a glorious fish that makes a good meal at any time of the year. It is best prepared very plainly so as not to disguise its flavor. Here, it is seasoned with salt and pepper and then broiled; piquant mustard cream sauce is spooned on afterward. A faintly sweet celery-root-and-apple puree makes a most pleasant accompaniment. Broccoli adds color to the plate; use the same steamer pot to cook the broccoli while you finish the puree. Serve rich, dense brownies chock-full of coconut for dessert.

Riesling will gracefully dance around the richness of the fish and its sauce. Each taste will remain fresh and complex because of riesling's flinty character.

BROILED SALMON WITH MUSTARD-CREAM SAUCE

The thick, center-cut salmon fillets work best here.

- ½ cup chicken stock or canned low-sodium chicken broth
- ¼ cup heavy cream
- 1 tablespoon Dijon mustard
  Salt and fresh-ground black pepper
- 12 ounces salmon fillet, cut into 2 pieces

1. Heat the broiler. In a small saucepan, bring the stock and cream to a boil over moderately high heat. Reduce the heat to moderate and simmer until reduced by half, about 5 minutes. Whisk in the mustard, season with salt and pepper, and bring just to a simmer. Cover and keep warm.

2. Sprinkle the salmon on both sides with salt and pepper. Broil

until just cooked through, about 4 minutes per side. Transfer the fillets to warmed plates, spoon the sauce on the fish, and serve.

—Stephanie Lyness

CELERY-ROOT-AND-APPLE PUREE
As you peel and cut the knobby celery root, drop the pieces into water with a little lemon juice to keep them from turning brown.

- 1 pound celery root, peeled and cut into chunks
- 2 large cloves garlic, peeled
- 1 small Golden Delicious apple, peeled, cored, and cut into chunks
- ⅓ cup milk
- 1½ teaspoons butter
- ½ teaspoon salt
- Fresh-ground black pepper

1. Steam the celery root and garlic in a steamer basket set over boiling water for 10 minutes. Add the apple and continue steaming until the celery root, garlic, and apple are very tender, about 5 minutes longer.

2. In a small saucepan, bring the milk to a boil. Transfer the celery-root mixture to a food processor or blender, add the hot milk, butter, and salt, and puree until smooth. Season with pepper and serve hot.

—Stephanie Lyness

COCONUT BROWNIES
This recipe makes sixteen brownies. Store leftovers in an airtight tin; they will keep for several days.

- 6 tablespoons unsalted butter
- 2 ounces unsweetened chocolate
- 1 cup sugar
- 2 eggs
- 1 teaspoon vanilla extract
- 1 cup flour

GAME PLAN

Heat the oven.

Mix and bake the brownies.

Steam the celery root and apple.

Reduce the cream sauce for the salmon.

Steam the broccoli.

Broil the salmon and finish the sauce.

1   teaspoon baking powder
¼   teaspoon salt
¾   cup sweetened shredded coconut

1. Heat the oven to 375°. Butter an 8-by-11½-inch baking dish.

2. In a double boiler, melt the butter and chocolate over warm water. Remove from the heat and stir in the sugar. Beat in the eggs one at a time. Stir in the vanilla.

3. In a small bowl, combine the flour, baking powder, and salt. Add to the chocolate mixture all at once and mix until incorporated. Stir in the coconut.

4. Scrape the batter into the prepared pan and smooth the surface. Bake for about 17 minutes, or until a knife inserted in the middle comes out clean. Do not overbake. Transfer the pan to a rack to cool; then cut the brownies into bars.

—STEPHANIE LYNESS

POLENTA TONIGHT

For a meatless meal, the robust combination of warm polenta and woodsy mushrooms is both satisfying and quick. Instant polenta, which cooks in five minutes, is a great alternative to the traditional long-cooking variety. Here it is enhanced with half-and-half and grated sharp cheddar and, to balance the richness, plenty of black pepper. The polenta is capped with a mushroom ragout accented with garlic, shallots, and a burst of parsley. A crunchy salad of bitter greens with a refreshing lemon and tarragon dressing complements the creamy main dish. For a no-fuss finale, sprinkle sliced ripe plums with sweet vermouth and serve cookies or biscotti on the side.

Earthy mushrooms and rich polenta (are there better flavors for fall?) will pair better with a minerally white than with a fat fruity one. A basic Chablis fits the bill perfectly, as would a dry Oregon riesling.

CHEDDAR-CHEESE POLENTA WITH MUSHROOM RAGOUT

Avoid orange cheddar for this recipe; use a sharp Vermont or New York State white cheddar instead.

2½ cups water
½ teaspoon salt
⅔ cup instant polenta
½ cup half-and-half
1½ to 2 teaspoons fresh-ground black pepper
1 cup shredded sharp cheddar (3 ounces)
  Mushroom Ragout (*recipe follows*)

1. Bring the water to a boil in a heavy medium saucepan. Add the salt. Gradually whisk in the polenta over moderate heat. Cook, stirring with a wooden spoon, until thickened and smooth, about 5 minutes.

2. Stir the half-and-half and pepper into the polenta. Remove from the heat and stir in the cheese. Spoon the polenta onto a warmed platter or individual plates and serve with the Mushroom Ragout.

—SUSAN COSTNER

MUSHROOM RAGOUT

This well-seasoned mix of mushrooms is also good over risotto.

¼ cup dried porcini mushrooms (¼ ounce)
¾ cup hot water
2 tablespoons butter
6 ounces assorted fresh mushrooms, such as cremini and shiitake, stems trimmed (or discarded if using shiitakes), large caps quartered or cut into thick slices
Salt and fresh-ground black pepper
1 tablespoon minced shallots
1 small clove garlic, minced
¼ cup chopped flat-leaf parsley

1. Put the porcinis in a small bowl and pour the hot water over them. Soak until softened, about 15 minutes.

2. Meanwhile, melt 1 tablespoon of the butter in a large heavy frying pan. Add half of the fresh mushrooms, season with salt and pepper, and cook over moderately high heat, stirring occasionally, until lightly browned, about 4 minutes. Transfer to a large plate. Repeat the process with the remaining 1 tablespoon of butter and the remaining fresh mushrooms, then return all the cooked mushrooms to the pan.

3. Drain the porcinis, reserving the soaking liquid. Rinse the porcinis well to remove any grit and then coarsely chop them and add to the pan along with the shallots and garlic. Cook over mod-

GAME PLAN

Soak the dried mushrooms.

Prepare the salad greens

Prepare the ragout ingredients; sauté the fresh mushrooms.

Cook the polenta.

Finish the mushroom ragout.

Toss the salad.

erate heat, stirring, for 3 minutes. Add the porcini liquid, stopping when you reach the grit at the bottom. Boil over high heat until reduced by half, about 4 minutes. Stir in the parsley and season with salt and pepper.

—SUSAN COSTNER

SALAD OF BITTER GREENS WITH LEMON TARRAGON DRESSING

  1 tablespoon minced fresh tarragon
1½ teaspoons lemon juice
  3 tablespoons olive oil
  1 small Belgian endive, cored and sliced
  1 small head radicchio, leaves separated
     Salt and fresh-ground black pepper

In a large glass or stainless-steel bowl, combine the tarragon and lemon juice. Gradually whisk in the oil. Add the endive and radicchio. Season with salt and pepper. Toss well and serve.

—SUSAN COSTNER

SOUTH-OF-THE-BORDER SHRIMP

Mexico's spicy cuisine does not have to be time-consuming: This simple dinner is ready with a few quick steps. For the main course, shrimp are sautéed in a tomato salsa with toasted anise and cumin seeds. Simmering corn in cream with sautéed poblano chile adds subtle heat. Aromatic steamed rice, made by placing sprigs of cilantro in the cooking water, absorbs the flavorful sauces. Mango sorbet or another favorite ice makes a palate-cooling dessert.

Fumé blanc from California, with ripe melon and oak flavors backed by sauvignon blanc's grassiness and acidity, will complement the shrimp and will not back down from the heat in this meal.

RANCH-STYLE SHRIMP

If you like a spicier dish, don't seed the jalapeño.

- ½ teaspoon aniseed
- ½ teaspoon cumin seeds
- 1 tablespoon cooking oil
- 2 scallions, sliced
- 2 cloves garlic, minced
- ½ pound plum tomatoes, chopped
- 1 jalapeño pepper, seeded and cut crosswise into thin rings
- ½ teaspoon dried oregano
- ½ teaspoon fresh-ground black pepper
- ¼ teaspoon salt
- ¾ pound medium shrimp, shelled
  Lime wedges, for serving

1. Heat a large heavy stainless-steel frying pan over moderately high heat. Add the anise and cumin seeds and toast, shaking the pan, until fragrant, about 1 minute. Transfer to a small bowl.

2. Heat the oil in the frying pan until almost smoking. Add the scallions and garlic and sauté over high heat, stirring, until softened but not browned, about 2 minutes. Add the tomatoes, jalapeño, oregano, black pepper, salt, and the toasted aniseed and cumin seeds, and cook for 2 more minutes. Stir in the shrimp and sauté, stirring occasionally, until pink, about 2 minutes. Transfer to plates and serve immediately, with lime wedges on the side.

—ZARELA MARTINEZ

CORN WITH POBLANO AND CREAM

If time allows, roast the chile over a gas flame or under the broiler until charred all over, then peel off the skin before chopping the chile.

1 tablespoon cooking oil
1 fresh poblano or Anaheim chile, seeded and minced
2 tablespoons minced onion
1 clove garlic, minced
1 cup frozen corn kernels, thawed
¼ cup light cream
1 tablespoon minced cilantro
¼ teaspoon salt

GAME PLAN

Shell the shrimp.

Start the rice.

Prepare the vegetables for sautéing and toast the spices.

Make the corn side dish.

Cook the shrimp.

Heat the oil in a small frying pan. Add the chile, onion, and garlic and sauté over moderately high heat, stirring frequently, until the onion is softened, about 4 minutes. Stir in the corn, cream, cilantro, and salt. Lower the heat to moderate and simmer until the cream is slightly thickened, about 3 minutes.

—ZARELA MARTINEZ

FALL'S FLAVORS

Pork, onions, potatoes, turnips, apples . . . a set of rather un-
assuming ingredients can be transformed into a lovely fall
menu. The pork chops bake on a bed of fennel-scented
sweetened onions. Grated potatoes and turnips slow-cook until
they become a crisp cake. If you are looking for a bit of color, add a
simple green salad. Cardamom, a spice used frequently in Scandi-
navian cooking, adds a delightful, heady scent to the dessert of
sautéed apples.

Ripe chardonnay from California or Australia will have the
fullness and texture to match well with this simple, robust
meal. Oak nuances and fruit weave nicely into the flavors and aromatics of the meat, onion, and fennel.

PORK CHOPS WITH RED ONIONS

*Today's pork is far leaner than the pork of ten or twenty years ago; take
care to not overcook it or it will dry out.*

2 teaspoons cooking oil
2 boneless pork loin chops (about 8 ounces each),
  ¾ to 1 inch thick, trimmed of excess fat
  Salt and fresh-ground black pepper
1 tablespoon butter
1 large red onion, sliced thin
½ teaspoon sugar
¼ teaspoon fennel seeds
1½ tablespoons wine vinegar
1 to 2 tablespoons water

1. Heat the oven to 375°. In a medium ovenproof frying pan, heat the oil over moderately high heat. Season the chops on both sides with salt and pepper; cook until lightly browned, about 2 minutes on each side. Transfer to a platter. Discard the fat and wipe out the pan.

2. In the same frying pan, melt the butter over moderate heat. Add the onion, sugar, and fennel seeds. Cook, stirring frequently, until the onion is softened and browned, 7 to 10 minutes. Add the vinegar and cook for 1 minute more, stirring. Season with salt and pepper to taste and stir in the water.

3. Place the chops on top of the onion mixture along with any of their accumulated juices. Cover and bake for about 15 minutes, until the chops are cooked through. Season the onion mixture with additional salt and pepper to taste and serve alongside the chops.

—STEPHANIE LYNESS

POTATO-AND-TURNIP CAKE

For a crisp cake, wipe dry the underside of the pan lid once or twice during cooking.

- 1 medium white turnip, peeled
- 1 large baking potato, peeled
- ½ teaspoon salt
- ¼ teaspoon fresh-ground black pepper
- 2 tablespoons cooking oil

1. Grate the turnip on the large holes of a box grater; transfer to a bowl. Then grate the potato and transfer to a bowl of cold water. Let soak for 1 minute.

2. Drain the potato and dry thoroughly with paper towels. Mix with the grated turnip. Season with the salt and pepper and toss well to combine.

3. In a medium nonstick or cast-iron frying pan, heat 1 tablespoon of the oil over moderately high heat. Add the potato-and-turnip mixture to the pan and press to pack evenly. Cover and cook, shaking the pan occasionally to keep the cake from sticking, until the bottom is golden brown, about 20 minutes.

GAME PLAN

Heat the oven.

Cook the potato-and-turnip cake.

Prepare the pork chops.

Make the salad.

Sauté the apples; you can rewarm them, adding the cream and cardamom at dessert time.

4. Invert a plate on top of the cake and flip the pan over to turn the cake out. Add the remaining tablespoon of oil to the frying pan and slide the cake back in, browned-side up. Continue to cook, uncovered, until the bottom is golden, about 20 minutes. Invert a serving plate over the pan, then flip the pan over to release the cake. Cut into quarters and serve immediately.

—STEPHANIE LYNESS

SAUTÉED APPLES WITH CREAM AND CARDAMOM

Although this dessert is delicious on its own, it can also be served with gingersnaps, vanilla wafers, or ice cream.

  1 tablespoon unsalted butter
  2 large Golden Delicious apples, peeled, cored, and sliced thin
1½ tablespoons sugar
 ¼ cup heavy cream
 ⅛ teaspoon ground cardamom
  1 tablespoon chopped walnuts

1. In a medium frying pan, melt the butter over high heat. Add the apples, sprinkle with the sugar, and cook, stirring frequently, until the apples have caramelized, 8 to 10 minutes. If the apples begin to burn, reduce the heat slightly. (*The recipe can be made to this point up to 30 minutes ahead.*)

2. Reduce the heat to moderate. Add the cream and cardamom and bring to a boil. Reduce the heat slightly and simmer for 1 minute. Sprinkle with the walnuts and serve immediately.

—STEPHANIE LYNESS

ORIENT EXPRESS

L overs of Asian food keep their kitchens stocked with an assortment of basic Asian ingredients—good soy sauce, fresh ginger, rice vinegar, sesame oil, chile oil, and two or three varieties of dried Asian noodles—so they can make delicious meals on a moment's notice. The menu here features cooked-in-a-flash chicken breasts flavored with a four-ingredient teriyaki glaze. Serve spicy-hot noodles with peanut sauce alongside. For a slightly crunchy salad, toss thinly sliced cucumbers in rice vinegar and salt and serve quite cold. Dress up bananas with ginger cooked in sugar.

With its own spiciness and full body and texture, gewürztraminer is justifiably the classic foil for spicy Asian dishes. But not any gewürztraminer: Some are sweet and flabby. A dry Alsace example is best, with Zind-Humbrecht being top-of-the-line.

TERIYAKI CHICKEN
The honey in the marinade gives the chicken a slight glaze.

    2 tablespoons sake or dry sherry
    2 tablespoons soy sauce
    1 tablespoon honey
    1 clove garlic, chopped
    2 boneless, skinless chicken breasts
       (about 6 ounces each)
    2 teaspoons cooking oil

1. In a medium bowl, whisk the sake, soy sauce, honey, and garlic. Add the chicken, turning to coat, and set aside in the refrigerator to marinate for 30 minutes.

2. Heat a heavy frying pan over high heat until very hot, about 2 minutes. Meanwhile, remove the chicken from the marinade. Add the oil to the pan and tilt it to coat. Reduce the heat to moderately high. Place the chicken in the pan with the small fillet of the breasts pushed to the side so that as much of the meat's surface as possible is exposed to direct heat. Cook, turning once, until browned, 7 to 8 minutes. Slice on the diagonal and serve.

—SUSAN SHAPIRO JASLOVE

NOODLES WITH SPICY PEANUT SAUCE

If you do not have soba (Japanese buckwheat) noodles, whole wheat spaghetti will work as a substitute.

    6   ounces soba noodles
    2   cups sliced Chinese cabbage
    ½   medium red bell pepper, cut into ¼-inch dice
    2   large scallions, including green tops,
        cut crosswise into thin slices
    ¼   cup smooth peanut butter
    2   tablespoons rice vinegar
    1¼ tablespoons soy sauce
    1   tablespoon honey
    1   teaspoon Asian sesame oil
    2   tablespoons water
        About 1 teaspoon chile oil
    ⅓   cup unsalted dry-roasted peanuts

1. Cook the noodles in a large pot of boiling water until just tender. Drain, rinse with cold water, and drain again. Transfer the noodles to a bowl. Add the cabbage, bell pepper, and scallions, and toss well.

2. In a medium bowl, whisk the peanut butter, vinegar, soy sauce, honey, and sesame oil until smooth. Whisk in the water. Add the chile oil, ¼ teaspoon at a time, to taste. Pour the dressing over the salad, sprinkle the peanuts on top, and toss well.

—SUSAN SHAPIRO JASLOVE

GAME PLAN

Marinate the chicken.

Prepare and chill the cucumbers.

Boil the water for the noodles.

Make the peanut sauce.

Cook the noodles and toss with the peanut sauce.

Cook the chicken.

Sauté the bananas right before serving the dessert.

GINGERED BANANAS

2 ripe, firm bananas
1 tablespoon unsalted butter
1 tablespoon light brown sugar
1½ teaspoons chopped fresh ginger
   Vanilla ice cream, for serving

1. Slice the bananas in half lengthwise. Slice each piece in half crosswise. Set aside.

2. In a large heavy frying pan, melt the butter over moderate heat. Add the brown sugar and stir to melt, about 15 seconds. Add the ginger and cook, stirring constantly, until the ginger releases its fragrance and begins to color, about 30 seconds.

3. Add the banana pieces and cook on one side until lightly browned, about 45 seconds. Flip over and brown the other side, another 45 seconds. Transfer the bananas to dessert plates, scraping up as much of the caramelized ginger as possible, and serve at once with ice cream.

—SUSAN SHAPIRO JASLOVE

A NEW TAKE
ON TUNA

E ven if you cannot be sitting in a café on the Promenade des Anglais overlooking the harbor in Nice, you certainly can enjoy the typically Niçoise flavors of tomatoes, garlic, olives, and anchovies. In this twist on the classic *salade niçoise*, pan-seared tuna steaks, green beans, and new potatoes are highly seasoned with a garlicky mustard anchovy vinaigrette. A fresh baguette is de rigueur. For the conclusion to the meal, serve either an imported or a domestic chèvre (goat cheese) and perfectly ripened Comice pears—a French favorite.

The meatiness of the tuna and the intensity of the mustard vinaigrette call out for red. Beaune reds—such as Pommard from Burgundy—will harmonize with the dish, as will the best of Oregon's pinot noirs.

SEARED-TUNA NIÇOISE SALAD

Searing develops color and flavor. For this recipe, buy tuna that has dark red meat, such as yellowfin.

  ¾ pound small new potatoes, cut into ¾-inch pieces
   1 tablespoon olive oil
  ½ pound green beans, trimmed and cut into 1-inch pieces
   2 5-ounce tuna steaks, about ½ inch thick
  ½ teaspoon fresh-ground black pepper
  ¼ teaspoon salt
     Mustard Anchovy Vinaigrette (*recipe follows*)
   1 medium tomato, cut into ½-inch dice (optional)
     Several Niçoise olives, for garnish

1. In a medium saucepan, cover the potatoes with salted water and bring to a boil over high heat. Boil until tender, about 10 minutes. Drain and reserve in a medium bowl.

2. Heat a medium heavy frying pan over moderately high heat. Add 1½ teaspoons of the oil and then the green beans; watch out for spattering. Stir-fry until lightly browned and crisp-tender, about 5 minutes. Remove the pan from the heat and transfer the beans to a bowl.

3. Season both sides of the tuna steaks with the pepper and salt. Return the frying pan to moderately high heat and add the remaining 1½ teaspoons oil. Add the tuna steaks and cook, turning once, until browned on the outside and cooked to taste, about 2 minutes per side for medium rare. Transfer the tuna to warm plates.

4. Toss half of the Mustard Anchovy Vinaigrette with the potatoes. Drizzle the remaining dressing over the tomato, if using, the green beans, and the tuna.

5. Neatly distribute the vegetables around the fish and top with the olives. Serve immediately.

—Susan Shapiro Jaslove

MUSTARD ANCHOVY VINAIGRETTE

```
1   teaspoon anchovy paste
1   clove garlic, minced, then mashed to a paste
1   teaspoon grainy mustard
1½  tablespoons red-wine vinegar
2   tablespoons olive oil
1   teaspoon capers, rinsed
    Salt and fresh-ground black pepper
```

In a small glass or stainless-steel bowl, whisk the anchovy paste with the garlic, mustard, and vinegar. Gradually whisk in the oil. Stir in the capers and season with salt and pepper.

—Susan Shapiro Jaslove

GAME PLAN

Boil the potatoes.

Whisk the vinaigrette.

Stir-fry the green beans.

Cook the tuna steaks.

Assemble the salad.

BRING ON THE RIBS

I f you became addicted to barbecuing meat, particularly ribs, this past summer, here is a meal to tide you over until it is time to dust off the grill again next June.

Succulent pork spareribs are the centerpiece of this dinner. They are coated with a sweet and hot maple-mustard glaze that takes about as much time to make as it does to open a bottle of commercial barbecue sauce. The ribs are baked and then finished under the broiler until they are brown and crisp. Thick potato wedges—seasoned with paprika, thyme, and cayenne-spiced oil—roast in the oven along with the spareribs. The coleslaw is a colorful assortment of green cabbage, red pepper, red onion, and carrot, tossed with a tangy yogurt-mayonnaise dressing.

A wedge of store-bought apple crumb pie, served à la mode if you like, makes a fitting dessert for this autumnal, all-American meal.

Consider a beer, of course, but if you prefer wine, buy one with firepower. Big, chewy California zinfandel or a similarly large Australian shiraz will have the weight to take on this hearty meal.

MAPLE-GLAZED SPARERIBS WITH SPICY FRIES

Use either country-style pork loin spareribs or the longer spareribs from the thick part of the belly. Cut the ribs into individual pieces; they take less time to cook than a slab of ribs. The potatoes can be kept warm in the oven while the ribs are broiling. Keep an eye on them so that they don't get too brown.

   2 large baking potatoes, halved crosswise and
       cut into ¾-inch-thick wedges
   1 tablespoon corn oil

½ teaspoon paprika
¼ teaspoon thyme
⅛ teaspoon cayenne
   Salt and fresh-ground black pepper
1½ pounds pork spareribs, cut into individual ribs
¼ teaspoon dried oregano, crumbled
2 tablespoons maple syrup, preferably dark amber
2 tablespoons spicy brown mustard
½ teaspoon white vinegar

1. Heat the oven to 375°. Place the potato wedges in a large baking dish or cast-iron frying pan. In a small bowl, whisk the oil with the paprika, thyme, cayenne, ¼ teaspoon salt, and pepper to taste. Drizzle the spicy oil over the potato wedges and toss to coat. Roast the potatoes in the upper third of the oven for about 40 minutes, turning occasionally, until tender inside and browned outside.

2. Meanwhile, put the ribs in a large roasting pan, season with salt and pepper, and sprinkle with the oregano. In a small bowl, whisk the maple syrup with the mustard and vinegar. Brush half the maple glaze over the ribs. Cover with aluminum foil and roast in the lower third of the oven for 30 to 40 minutes, turning occasionally, until cooked through.

3. Heat the broiler. Brush the ribs with the remaining maple glaze. Broil, uncovered, for about 5 minutes, turning once, until nicely browned and glazed. Divide the ribs and potato wedges between two large plates and serve at once.

—TRACEY SEAMAN

CONFETTI SLAW

1 tablespoon mustard seeds
½ pound green cabbage, cored and shredded
1 small carrot, peeled and grated
1 small red bell pepper, diced
½ small red onion, diced
⅓ cup cilantro leaves, chopped
3 tablespoons plain yogurt

GAME PLAN

Heat the oven.

Prepare and begin to roast the potatoes.

Make the maple glaze, brush it on the ribs and bake them.

Prepare the coleslaw.

Broil the ribs.

2 tablespoons mayonnaise
½ teaspoon sugar
  Salt and fresh-ground black pepper

1. In a small dry frying pan, toast the mustard seeds over moderate heat, stirring occasionally, until they pop and turn brown, about 2 minutes.

2. In a large bowl, toss the cabbage with the carrot, bell pepper, red onion, cilantro, and mustard seeds. In a small bowl, whisk the yogurt with the mayonnaise, sugar, and ¼ teaspoon each of salt and pepper. Spoon the dressing over the vegetables and toss well. Season with salt and pepper and serve.

—TRACEY SEAMAN

FOOLPROOF FISH

A hearty quick-cooking ragout of vegetables and a little white wine forms a savory bed for pan-poached bluefish fillets. Because the vegetables are juicy, there is no need to make a sauce. Just lay the fish on top of them, cover the pan, and let the cooking take its course. This recipe works just as well with other fish or with chicken breasts or pork loin. All that is left to do is make the zesty orzo accompaniment and the simple dessert.

From the mouth of the Loire River in France comes Muscadet de Sèvre-et-Maine *sur lie*. Aged on the lees (dead yeast cells), which impart a light doughy aroma, Muscadet is a light, high-acid wine that will easily cut the oiliness of the fish.

ONE-DISH BLUEFISH

The relatively high oil content of bluefish makes it quite perishable. Buy the freshest fillets you can find and cook them the day of or the day following purchase.

½ pound sweet potatoes, peeled and cut into 2-inch chunks
3 tablespoons olive oil
4 scallions, including green tops, cut into 1-inch pieces
1 clove garlic, minced
¼ cup dry white wine
¾ cup canned chopped tomatoes in puree
½ teaspoon ground cardamom
    Salt and fresh-ground black pepper
2 skin-on bluefish fillets (about 7 ounces each)
1 tablespoon minced flat-leaf parsley

1. Put the sweet potatoes in a food processor and pulse until the largest pieces are about ½ inch and the smallest about ¼ inch. Set the sweet potatoes aside.

2. In a deep stainless-steel frying pan, heat the oil. Add the scallions and cook over moderately high heat, stirring, until just softened, about 3 minutes. Add the garlic and cook, stirring, until fragrant, about 1 minute. Pour in the wine, bring to a boil, and boil for 1 minute. Add the sweet potatoes, tomatoes, cardamom, 1 teaspoon salt, and a generous grinding of pepper. Reduce the heat to moderate, cover, and cook until the potatoes are just tender, about 20 minutes.

3. Using tweezers or pliers, remove the small pin bones that run the length of the bluefish fillets. Season the fillets with salt and pepper and arrange them, skin-side down, on top of the vegetable ragout, overlapping them slightly if necessary. Sprinkle the bluefish with the parsley, cover, and cook until the fish begins to flake, about 15 minutes. Transfer the bluefish fillets and the vegetable ragout to serving plates, spoon some of the cooking juices over the fish, and serve.

—PAUL GRIMES

LEMON PARMESAN ORZO

⅔ cup orzo
⅓ cup chicken stock or canned low-sodium chicken broth
1 teaspoon minced lemon zest
½ teaspoon dried thyme
½ teaspoon salt
¼ teaspoon fresh-ground black pepper
2 teaspoons butter
¼ cup grated Parmesan

Cook the orzo in a saucepan of boiling, salted water until just done, 8 to 10 minutes. Drain the orzo and return it to the pan. Add the stock, lemon zest, thyme, salt, and pepper. Cook over moderately high heat, stirring occasionally, until most of the liquid is absorbed. Stir in the butter and Parmesan just before serving.

—PAUL GRIMES

GAME PLAN

Chill dessert glasses and blender canister.

Cut up and cook vegetables for the fish.

Start water for the orzo.

Cook the fish and orzo.

Finish the orzo.

Make the green salad.

Make the ice-cream parfaits just before serving.

RUM SMOOTHIE PARFAITS

Before dinner, put two wineglasses and the blender canister in the freezer to chill and prepare the ingredients for the parfaits. Make the dessert immediately before serving it.

2 tablespoons rum, preferably dark
½ pint hard-frozen vanilla ice cream
¼ cup golden raisins or any dried fruit
2 teaspoons nuts, such as almonds or pecans, chopped fine
2 sprigs fresh mint
Crisp sugar cookies (optional)

1. Add the rum to the ice-cold blender canister and scoop in the ice cream. Blend for 20 to 30 seconds, or until smooth, stopping now and then to break up and stir in the lumps.

2. Pour the softened ice cream into the chilled wineglasses and sprinkle the ice cream with the raisins and nuts. Top the parfaits with the mint sprigs. Serve with crisp sugar cookies, if desired.

—PAUL GRIMES

QUAIL, QUICKLY

Quail is always a popular item in restaurants—not only with diners who like its taste, but also with the kitchen staff because it is easy to prepare and quick to cook. For the same reasons, quail is terrific for a weekday dinner. And, very much to the point, the birds are also now readily available at butcher shops and many supermarkets.

Sautéed potatoes accompany game well, and the slight bitterness of the sautéed watercress balances the sweetness of the honey-glazed quail. To finish, dress up a bowl of bananas and store-bought vanilla ice cream with caramel sauce.

Normally quail dishes require a white wine, but the honey in this meal would make an acidic white feel tart. A ripe, low-tannin California or Chile merlot will mesh best with the glaze.

HONEY-GLAZED QUAIL

Only a small amount of honey goes into this dish and so the sweetness is subtle; it rounds out the flavor of the sauce rather than making it cloying.

4 quail
   Salt and fresh-ground black pepper
1 tablespoon plus 1 teaspoon butter
2 teaspoons olive oil
2 teaspoons honey
2 tablespoons water

1. With poultry shears, snip down both sides of the backbone of a quail. Discard the backbone. Repeat with the remaining quail. Flatten the quail gently with the heel of your hand. Season them lightly with salt and pepper.

2. In a large frying pan, melt the 1 tablespoon of butter with the oil and 1 teaspoon of the honey over moderately high heat. Add the quail, skin-side down, and cook until well browned, about 5 minutes. Turn, cover, and cook until the juices run clear when the thigh is pierced with a knife, about 5 minutes longer. Arrange two quail on each plate.

3. Add the water and the remaining 1 teaspoon honey to the pan and boil until thickened, about 1 minute. Whisk in the remaining 1 teaspoon butter. Season with salt and pepper to taste, spoon over the quail, and serve.

—STEPHANIE LYNESS

SAUTÉED POTATOES WITH THYME

3 medium boiling potatoes (about 12 ounces)
2 teaspoons butter
2 teaspoons olive oil
½ teaspoon chopped fresh thyme, plus some sprigs for garnish
Salt and fresh-ground black pepper

1. In a pot of boiling salted water, cook the potatoes until just tender, about 20 minutes. Drain and cut into ½-inch chunks.

2. In a medium frying pan, melt the butter with the oil over moderately high heat. Add the potatoes and sauté, shaking the pan occasionally, for 4 minutes. Add the chopped thyme and season with salt and pepper to taste. Sauté until the potatoes are lightly browned, about 3 minutes. Garnish the potatoes with thyme sprigs and serve.

—STEPHANIE LYNESS

SAUTÉED WATERCRESS WITH WALNUTS

1½ teaspoons olive oil
1 large bunch watercress, large stems removed
Salt and fresh-ground black pepper
1 tablespoon chopped walnuts

GAME PLAN

Boil the potatoes.

Make the caramel sauce.

Sauté the quail, the potatoes, and the watercress.

Finish the honey glaze just before serving.

197

In a large frying pan, heat the oil over moderately high heat. Add the watercress and sauté until wilted, 1 to 2 minutes. Season with salt and pepper to taste. Sprinkle with the walnuts and serve hot.

—STEPHANIE LYNESS

VANILLA SUNDAES WITH CARAMEL SAUCE

Never leave caramel cooking unattended on the stove; it can go from pale golden to burnt sugar very quickly.

½ cup sugar
¼ cup plus 1 tablespoon water
¼ cup heavy cream
  Vanilla ice cream
1 banana, quartered

1. In a medium saucepan, combine the sugar and the ¼ cup of water. Cook, stirring, over low heat until the sugar is dissolved, 1 to 2 minutes. Increase the heat to moderate and let cook until the caramel is a dark amber, about 15 minutes.

2. Remove the caramel from the heat and immediately stir in the cream and the remaining 1 tablespoon water. Return the sauce to low heat and whisk until smooth. Remove from the heat and let cool slightly.

3. Scoop some ice cream into two bowls. Place two banana quarters on either side of the ice cream and pour some caramel sauce (warm or at room temperature) on top. Serve immediately.

—STEPHANIE LYNESS

A Speedy Fiesta

S avory pies can make memorable—and fast—dinners. Mexican tamales, a popular fiesta food, served as the inspiration for a quick frying-pan pie, which uses polenta as the base to hold a spicy black-bean filling. Traditional tamales are made of cornmeal mush that is wrapped and steamed in cornhusks—a process that can take hours. Instant polenta yields the same distinctive cornmeal flavor and is ready in five minutes. An avocado salad and chocolate custards continue the Mexican theme.

Consider a Spanish wine to go with this Mexican food. A young red Rioja of medium weight will round out the savory polenta pie, with its aromatic cumin and mild heat. For a little more fruit, try a red from Ribera del Duero.

MEXICAN POLENTA PIE
Cooked, shredded chicken or pork are good alternatives to the black beans.

- 1 tablespoon cooking oil
- 1 small onion, chopped
- 4 ounces mushrooms, sliced thin
- ½ teaspoon cumin seeds
- ½ teaspoon chili powder
- ¼ teaspoon dried red-pepper flakes
- 1 14-ounce can plum tomatoes, drained
- 1 4-ounce can chopped mild green chiles, drained
- 1 cup cooked black beans, rinsed if canned
- ½ teaspoon salt
- 1½ cups water
- ½ cup instant polenta
- ¼ cup grated sharp cheddar

199

1. Heat the oven to 400°. In a large stainless-steel frying pan, heat the oil over moderately high heat. Add the onion and cook, stirring occasionally, until slightly softened, about 3 minutes. Add the mushrooms, cumin seeds, chili powder, and red-pepper flakes. Cook, stirring occasionally, until the mushrooms soften and release juices, about 3 minutes.

2. Crush the tomatoes and add them to the frying pan. Stir in the green chiles and black beans. Reduce the heat to moderate and simmer for at least 10 minutes. Stir in ¼ teaspoon of the salt.

3. Meanwhile, in a small ovenproof frying pan, combine the water and the remaining ¼ teaspoon salt. Bring to a boil over high heat and stir in the polenta. Reduce the heat to moderately high and cook, stirring, until the polenta holds its shape, about 5 minutes. Remove from the heat and smooth the polenta evenly in the pan. Set aside for 5 minutes.

4. Spread the black-bean chili over the polenta. Sprinkle the cheese on top. Bake for 12 to 15 minutes, until the chili is bubbling and the cheese is melted. Let stand for 15 minutes before serving.

—SUSAN SHAPIRO JASLOVE

AVOCADO-AND-ROMAINE SALAD

- 1 tablespoon lime juice
- 1 small clove garlic, minced
- ½ teaspoon grainy mustard
- ½ teaspoon honey
- 1 tablespoon cooking oil
- 1 ripe avocado, preferably Hass, cut into ½-inch dice
  Salt and fresh-ground black pepper
- ½ small head romaine lettuce, torn into 2-inch pieces

In a small glass or stainless-steel bowl, whisk the lime juice with the garlic, mustard, and honey. Whisk in the oil and the diced avocado. Season with salt and pepper to taste. Place the lettuce in a serving bowl, add the avocado dressing, and toss.

—SUSAN SHAPIRO JASLOVE

GAME PLAN

Heat the oven.

Bake the custards.

Prepare the polenta pie; while it bakes, make the salad.

INDIVIDUAL BAKED CHOCOLATE CUSTARDS

For authentic Mexican chocolate flavor, dust the baked custards with a little cinnamon.

¾ cup milk
1 tablespoon plus 1 teaspoon cocoa powder
2 tablespoons dark brown sugar
  Pinch salt
1 egg, at room temperature
¼ teaspoon vanilla extract

1. Heat the oven to 350°. Place two 6-ounce ramekins or custard cups in an 8-inch-square baking pan.

2. In a small saucepan, whisk the milk and cocoa until combined. Bring to a boil over moderately high heat, stirring occasionally with a wooden spoon.

3. In a medium bowl, combine the brown sugar and salt. Whisk in the egg and vanilla until thoroughly combined. Whisk about one-quarter of the hot chocolate milk into the egg mixture. Pour the remaining chocolate milk into the egg mixture in a steady stream, stirring gently with a rubber spatula until blended.

4. Pour the custard into the ramekins. Fill the baking pan with enough warm water to reach halfway up the side of the ramekins. Bake for 22 minutes, or until the custards are just set but still slightly wobbly in the center. Remove the ramekins from the water and set aside to cool. Serve the custards at room temperature or refrigerate until chilled.

—Susan Shapiro Jaslove

HEARTY SOUP

The first hard frost has killed the last of the tomatoes in the garden and there are pumpkins piling up at market stands—sure signs that it is time to make a hot soup for dinner. This one of Italian sausages, fennel, spinach, and orzo will warm you up nicely, and it is so hearty all you need is a slice or two of your favorite bread alongside. Baked pears are an appropriate fall ending.

Good Chianti Rufina tends to have a little more power than most Chianti Classico and will stand up to this hearty soup. To turn up the intensity of the wine, try an Amarone della Valpolicella, with its deep flavors and hints of raisins.

FENNEL-AND-TOMATO SOUP WITH ITALIAN SAUSAGES

For less spice, use all mild Italian sausages.

   2 teaspoons olive oil
   1 small bulb fennel, diced
   1 small onion, diced
   1 clove garlic, minced
   2 teaspoons tomato paste
2½ cups chicken stock or canned low-sodium chicken broth
   ¾ cup canned Italian plum tomatoes with their juices,
      tomatoes chopped
      Salt and fresh-ground black pepper
   ¼ pound mild Italian sausage
   ¼ pound hot Italian sausage
   ½ cup orzo
   1 cup torn spinach leaves

1. In a large stainless-steel saucepan, heat the oil. Add the fennel and onion; cook over moderate heat, stirring, until the onion is translucent and beginning to brown, about 5 minutes. Add the garlic; cook, stirring, until fragrant, about 1 minute. Blend in the tomato paste. Add the stock and the tomatoes with their juices. Season with salt and pepper; bring to a simmer. Reduce the heat, cover, and simmer gently for 20 minutes.

2. Meanwhile, heat a heavy frying pan. Prick the sausages all over with a fork and add to the pan. Cook over moderately low heat. turning, until browned and cooked through, about 20 minutes. Drain on paper towels and let cool slightly. Halve the sausages lengthwise, then cut them into ½-inch pieces.

3. Bring the soup to a boil, add the orzo, and cook, stirring occasionally, until just done, about 10 minutes. Add the spinach and sausages and cook, stirring, until the spinach is wilted and the sausages are heated through, 2 to 3 minutes.

—JUDITH SUTTON

BAKED PEARS

2 firm but ripe Bartlett pears
1½ tablespoons light brown sugar
1 tablespoon chopped candied ginger
2 teaspoons unsalted butter
2 tablespoons pecan pieces
Vanilla ice cream or frozen yogurt, for serving

Heat the oven to 350°. Peel and halve the pears. With a small spoon or melon baller, scoop out the seeds. Butter an 8-inch-square baking dish and put in the pear halves, cut-side up. Sprinkle the pears with the brown sugar and candied ginger. Dot with the butter and scatter the pecan pieces on top. Bake on the top shelf of the oven until hot and bubbling, about 20 minutes. Serve immediately with ice cream.

—SARAH FRITSCHNER

GAME PLAN

Prepare the soup.

Bake the pears.

CHICKEN IN A BUN

When was the last time you ate a really good fast-food meal? One in which the burger was juicy and the fries were hot and crisp? Our take on burgers and fries is guaranteed to taste fresher and be healthier for you than anything you might pick up at the drive-through window. The "burger" features a quickly seared chicken breast topped with a lemony tahini sauce. The fries are actually roasted, and they are *sweet* potatoes, which crisp up wonderfully in a very hot oven. You can splurge on a grown-up sundae for dessert. So pull up the swivel stools to the kitchen counter, tune the radio to the oldies station, sit down, and dig in.

There are some great inexpensive chardonnays coming out of Chile right now. The area to watch is Casablanca, a slightly cooler area producing whites with good fruit and finesse—elements for a perfect pairing with this easy menu.

SESAME CHICKEN IN A BUN

2 tablespoons dry bread crumbs
1 tablespoon sesame seeds
  Salt
  Pinch cayenne
2 boneless, skinless chicken breasts, slightly flattened
1 tablespoon cooking oil
2 crusty rolls
  Several sprigs watercress, large stems removed
2 tomato slices (optional)
¼ cup Lemon Sesame Sauce (*recipe follows*)
1 tablespoon Asian sesame oil

1. In a plastic bag, combine the bread crumbs, sesame seeds, salt, and cayenne; shake until blended. One at a time, add the chicken breasts to the bag and shake to coat.

2. In a medium heavy frying pan, heat the oil over moderately high heat. Add the chicken and fry until golden brown, about 5 minutes. Turn the chicken and fry until golden and cooked through, about 5 minutes longer.

3. Meanwhile, place an opened roll on each dinner plate. Arrange a few sprigs of watercress and a tomato slice, if using, on the bottom half of each roll. Spread a heaping tablespoon of the Lemon Sesame Sauce on the top half of each roll. Place the chicken breasts on the sauced half; drizzle some sesame oil on top and serve.

LEMON SESAME SAUCE

If you have not used all the sauce for the chicken, serve it on the side as a dip for the sweet potatoes.

- ¼ cup tahini (sesame paste)
- 3 tablespoons lemon juice
- ¼ cup water
- ¼ teaspoon salt

In a small bowl, mix the tahini and lemon juice. Slowly mix in the water until the sauce is smooth and creamy. Season with the salt.

—SUSAN SHAPIRO JASLOVE

ROASTED SWEET POTATOES

- 2 teaspoons cooking oil
- 1 pound sweet potatoes, unpeeled, cut into sticks
  Salt and fresh-ground black pepper

Heat the oven to 500°. Spread the oil over the bottom of a large rimmed baking sheet. Spread the sweet potatoes in the pan; they should not touch. Bake on the bottom rack of the oven for 10 to 15 minutes until browned. Season with salt and pepper to taste.

—SUSAN SHAPIRO JASLOVE

GAME PLAN

Heat the oven.

Make the sauce.

Cut the sweet potatoes and roast.

Sauté the chicken breasts.

Toast the almonds.

Assemble the dessert just before serving.

TOASTED ALMOND FREEZE

This was inspired by a toasted almond cocktail, which is a mixture of Kahlúa, amaretto, and cream.

2 tablespoons sliced almonds
1 tablespoon coffee liqueur, preferably Kahlúa
1 tablespoon amaretto
   Vanilla ice cream

1. Heat the oven to 500°. In a small baking pan, toast the almonds until lightly browned, about 2 minutes.

2. In a small bowl, combine the coffee liqueur and the amaretto. Scoop the ice cream into small dessert bowls. Pour the liqueur mixture on top and sprinkle with the toasted almonds.

—SUSAN SHAPIRO JASLOVE

THE MENU

Pork Stew with
Garlic and Escarole

Crusty Bread

Apple Pecan Crisp

A SAVORY STEW

Technically, a stew should cook for a long time to tenderize the typically tough meat and meld the varied flavors. But after a long day at the office, slow-cooking stews are hardly an option. For this satisfying fall menu, we chose pork tenderloin, which cooks to tenderness in mere minutes. It quickly stews in a soupy broth redolent of rosemary and wine. A big loaf of crusty bread will sop up the broth. For dessert, there is apple crisp, a perennial fall favorite.

A young white Rioja from a modern producer (such the widely available Marqués de Cáceres) has a clean, round apple flavor and citric acidity, both of which complement the pork.

PORK STEW WITH GARLIC AND ESCAROLE
Pork tenderloin is nearly as lean as chicken breast, and like chicken, it becomes dry if overcooked.

- 1   pork tenderloin (about ¾ pound), trimmed and cut into ½-inch-thick slices
      Salt and fresh-ground black pepper
- 1   tablespoon olive oil
- 2   cloves garlic, crushed
- 1   medium onion, chopped
- ¼   teaspoon dried rosemary, crumbled
- 2   tablespoons dry white wine
- ¾   pound red potatoes, cut into small cubes
- 1¼   cups chicken stock or canned low-sodium chicken broth
- 2½   cups torn escarole

1. Season the pork with salt and pepper. In a heavy Dutch oven, heat ½ tablespoon of the oil. Brown the pork over high heat, about 2 minutes per side; transfer to a plate.

2. Add the remaining ½ tablespoon oil to the pan; reduce the heat. Add the garlic and cook, mashing and stirring it, until soft and golden, about 4 minutes. Add the onion and rosemary. Cook, stirring, until the onion softens, about 5 minutes. Add the wine; simmer until almost evaporated, about 4 minutes. Add the potatoes and stock; season with salt and pepper. Bring to a boil, cover, and boil gently until the potatoes are tender, about 20 minutes.

3. Add the pork to the stew; simmer for 2 minutes. Add the escarole and cook, stirring, until it is wilted but still bright green and the pork is cooked through, about 2 minutes. Serve hot.

—JUDITH SUTTON

THINKING AHEAD

Pork tenderloins often come in packages of two. We suggest that, instead of freezing the extra meat, you make a double batch of pork stew up to the point of adding the escarole (escarole does not freeze well). Freeze half of the stew with a note taped to the container to remind yourself to stir two and a half cups torn escarole into the stew before serving.

GAME PLAN

Heat the oven.

Brown the pork and simmer the vegetables for the stew.

Assemble and bake the apple crisp.

Finish the stew.

APPLE PECAN CRISP

Choose a tart yet flavorful apple for this crisp: Cortland, Northern Spy, or Rhode Island Greening are all superb, and Granny Smith will do in a pinch.

⅓ cup pecans
2 tablespoons flour
2 tablespoons light brown sugar
¼ cup granulated sugar
2 tablespoons cold unsalted butter, cut into ½-inch dice

2½ tablespoons rolled oats
 2 large tart cooking apples, peeled, cored, and sliced
 2 tablespoons dried cranberries
    Vanilla ice cream, for serving

1. Heat the oven to 350°. Spread the pecans on a baking sheet and bake for 6 to 8 minutes, or until lightly toasted. Let the nuts cool, then coarsely chop them. Leave the oven on.

2. In a small bowl, combine the flour, brown sugar, and 2 table-spoons of the granulated sugar. Work in the butter with your fin-gertips until the mixture resembles coarse meal. Stir in the toasted pecans and the oats.

3. Generously butter two individual baking dishes; they should be about 6 inches wide and 1 inch deep. In a medium bowl, toss the apples with the cranberries and the remaining 2 tablespoons granulated sugar. Divide the apple mixture between the prepared baking dishes and cover with the topping. Set the dishes on a large baking sheet and bake in the bottom third of the oven for 35 to 40 minutes, or until the apples are tender when pierced and the top-ping is toasted. Serve warm with the ice cream.

—JAMES HENAHAN

SPANISH-STYLE FISH FILLETS

The sunny cuisine of southern Spain's Andalusian region is marked by an abundance of fish and produce. Arabic spices found in many of the dishes are a reminder of the centuries of Muslim presence there. This early fall dinner features baked white-fleshed fish swathed in a mellow sauce of potato, tomato, and bell pepper enhanced with cumin. The accompanying sautéed lima beans benefit from the exquisite bite of cured ham. Juicy sliced oranges sprinkled with shredded coconut and topped with a dollop of whipped cream make an easy way to end the meal.

Continue the Mediterranean theme by sailing over to Sardinia in Italy for a vermentino. Good examples are aromatic and crisp, making them perfect with seafood. If you cannot find one, head to mainland Italy for pinot bianco.

ANDALUSIAN BAKED FISH

The sauce for this fish, typical of those found in the Sierra Morena area, is called potato sauce, *although very little potato is actually used.*

¼ cup olive oil
1 small all-purpose potato, peeled and chopped
1 medium red bell pepper, chopped
1 medium tomato, peeled, seeded, and chopped
½ cup water
¼ teaspoon cumin seeds
1 bay leaf
 Salt and fresh-ground black pepper
2 cod or hake fillets (about 5 ounces each),
 about ½ inch thick

1. Heat the oven to 400°. Heat the oil in a large stainless-steel frying pan. Add the potato and cook over moderate heat, stirring occasionally, for 5 minutes. Add the bell pepper and tomato and cook, stirring, until soft, about 10 minutes.

2. Stir the water into the vegetables along with the cumin seeds, bay leaf, ½ teaspoon salt, and ⅛ teaspoon pepper. Bring to a boil over moderately high heat. Lower the heat and simmer briskly, stirring occasionally, until the potato is tender, about 10 minutes.

3. Arrange the cod fillets in a lightly oiled baking dish and season with salt and pepper. Bake for about 8 minutes, until the fish is opaque and flakes easily. Cover with aluminum foil and keep warm.

4. Meanwhile, pass the potato sauce through a food mill or coarse strainer and return it to the frying pan. Simmer over moderate heat, stirring, until thickened, about 8 minutes. Season with salt and pepper.

5. Transfer the cod fillets to individual plates. Spoon the potato sauce over the fish and serve.

—CLIFFORD A. WRIGHT

SAUTÉED LIMA BEANS WITH PROSCIUTTO

Prosciutto stands in for the traditional jamón serrano, *the cured ham used extensively in Andalusia.*

1 cup frozen baby lima beans
1½ teaspoons olive oil
1 ounce prosciutto, diced
   Salt and fresh-ground black pepper

1. Cook the lima beans in a medium saucepan of boiling, salted water until tender, about 10 minutes. Drain.

2. Heat the oil in a medium saucepan. Add the prosciutto and stir over moderate heat until beginning to brown, about 2 minutes. Add the lima beans and cook, tossing occasionally, until heated through, about 3 minutes. Season with salt and pepper.

—CLIFFORD A. WRIGHT

GAME PLAN

Heat the oven.

Macerate the oranges.

Start the sauce for the fish.

Boil the lima beans and sauté them.

Bake the fish.

Finish the sauce.

Whip the cream right before serving dessert.

SLICED ORANGES WITH COCONUT

The combination of oranges, coconut, and cream may sound unlikely, but the resulting flavor brings back sweet memories of orange Creamsicles.

2 Valencia or navel oranges
1 tablespoon sugar
¼ cup sweetened shredded coconut
⅓ cup heavy cream, whipped to soft peaks

1. Peel the oranges with a sharp knife, discarding all the bitter white pith. Slice the oranges crosswise ⅜ inch thick and arrange the slices, overlapping them slightly, on a serving platter. Sprinkle with the sugar and let stand for 30 minutes.

2. Sprinkle the coconut over the orange slices and serve with the whipped cream.

—CLIFFORD A. WRIGHT

PORK WITH STYLE

T oday's meat and potatoes have a lot more style than their stodgy counterparts of decades past. Here, tender pork medallions are quickly sautéed, flavored with a dash of balsamic vinegar, and garnished with prosciutto, plum tomatoes, and arugula. Creamy potatoes mashed with Parmesan and topped with rosemary butter offer a delicious contrast to the zesty pork. Steamed green beans need no embellishment with these colorful flavors on the plate. For dessert, dress up orange sorbet with a sprinkling of chopped pistachios.

A tannic red would overwhelm the lean pork medallions here. Dolcetto is characteristically low in tannin, however, with plenty of fruit to balance the salty prosciutto. Renato Ratti and Aldo Conterno are excellent producers.

PORK MEDALLIONS WITH ARUGULA AND TOMATOES
Bright Italian flavors—salty prosciutto, spicy arugula, and succulent tomatoes—combine in an exciting topping for the sautéed pork.

  1 tablespoon olive oil
2½ ounces thin slices of prosciutto, chopped
  1 clove garlic, minced
  1 pork tenderloin (about ¾ pound), trimmed and
     sliced into 1-inch-thick medallions
  1 tablespoon balsamic vinegar
 ½ pound arugula, large stems removed, leaves chopped
 ½ pound plum tomatoes, chopped
     Salt and fresh-ground black pepper

1. Heat the oil in a large stainless-steel frying pan. Add the prosciutto and garlic and cook over moderate heat, stirring, until the garlic is golden, about 3 minutes. Transfer to a plate.

2. Add the pork medallions to the pan and cook over high heat until well browned on the outside and medium inside, 3 to 4 minutes per side. Transfer the cooked pork to a serving platter and keep warm.

3. Add the vinegar to the pan and boil for 1 minute, scraping up any brown bits. Add the arugula and cook, stirring, until wilted, about 2 minutes. Add the tomatoes and the prosciutto mixture. Cook over high heat for 2 minutes, stirring occasionally. Season with salt and pepper. Spoon the mixture over the pork and serve.

—Nancy Verde Barr

PARMESAN MASHED POTATOES

Rinse dried rosemary in hot water before mixing it with the butter.

- 2 tablespoons butter, at room temperature
- 1½ teaspoons chopped fresh rosemary, or
  - ½ teaspoon dried rosemary
- 1 pound baking potatoes, peeled and cut into 1-inch dice
  Salt
- ¼ cup warm milk
- ¼ cup grated Parmesan
  Fresh-ground black pepper

1. In a small bowl, blend the butter with the rosemary. In a medium saucepan, cover the potatoes with cold water and stir in ½ teaspoon salt. Bring to a boil over moderately high heat. Boil until the potatoes are tender, about 15 minutes. Drain well and return to the pan.

2. Add the warm milk and Parmesan to the potatoes and mash them with a potato masher or hand-held electric mixer. Season with salt and pepper and serve topped with the rosemary butter.

—Nancy Verde Barr

GAME PLAN

Boil the potatoes.

Prepare the topping for the pork.

Steam the green beans.

Mash the potatoes.

Sauté the pork.

A DECADENT BALANCE

There are times when you have to work backward in menu planning. If, for instance, you want to put considerable effort into the dessert, you would like the main course to be as swift and simple as possible, as is the case in the menu here. The dessert is bittersweet chocolate bombes; barely sweet and undeniably rich, it calls for a boldly flavored yet uncomplicated main course. The light but flavor-packed sauce for the linguine is ready in the time it takes to boil the water and cook the pasta. Italian bread and a plainly dressed salad are the only other accompaniments you will need.

For the main course, a simple Chianti or dolcetto will suffice. Spoil yourself for dessert with a half bottle of Muscat de Beaumes-de-Venise, a Rhône dessert wine redolent of honey and apricots. Feeling *really* decadent? Try a Sauternes instead.

LINGUINE WITH BITTER GREENS AND PANCETTA
Pancetta adds a salty edge to this dish. The flavorful Italian bacon is cured in salt and spices and comes in a sausagelike roll. You will find it at Italian markets and well-stocked delis.

  2 tablespoons olive oil
1½ teaspoons minced garlic
  1 ounce pancetta, cut into ¼-inch dice
⅛ teaspoon dried red-pepper flakes
1½ cups chicken stock or canned low-sodium chicken broth
½ pound dried linguine or spaghetti
  1 small bunch arugula, shredded (about 2 cups)
  3 tablespoons grated Parmesan

1. In a large frying pan, combine the oil, garlic, pancetta, and red-pepper flakes and cook over high heat until the garlic is golden. Add the stock and bring to a boil. Lower the heat to moderately high and boil gently until the liquid is reduced by half, about 6 minutes.

2. Meanwhile, in a large pot of boiling, salted water, cook the linguine until just done, about 12 minutes. Drain the linguine, reserving ¼ cup of the pasta-cooking water.

3. Add the linguine to the frying pan and cook over moderate heat, tossing occasionally, until just done. Add the reserved pasta-cooking water, 1 tablespoon at a time, if the linguine seems dry. Fold in the arugula, transfer to a bowl and sprinkle with the Parmesan. Serve immediately.

—JOHANNE KILLEEN AND GEORGE GERMON

BALSAMIC VINAIGRETTE

2 tablespoons olive oil
2 teaspoons balsamic vinegar
½ teaspoon minced fresh oregano
¼ teaspoon minced garlic
 Salt and fresh-ground black pepper

In a small glass or stainless-steel bowl, combine the oil, vinegar, oregano, and garlic. Season with salt and pepper and whisk to blend.

—CHRIS SCHLESINGER AND JOHN WILLOUGHBY

BITTERSWEET CHOCOLATE BOMBES

If you like decadent cakes with runny centers, cut the cooking time to about fifteen minutes.

3 ounces bittersweet chocolate, coarsely chopped
4 tablespoons unsalted butter
1 large egg
1 large egg yolk
⅓ cup granulated sugar
⅓ cup flour
1 teaspoon confectioners' sugar

GAME PLAN

Heat the oven.

Mix and bake the chocolate bombes.

Put a large pot of water on to boil for the linguine.

Prepare the romaine for the salad.

Make the sauce and boil the linguine.

Mix the vinaigrette and toss the salad.

Toss the pasta ingredients with the sauce and arugula.

1. Heat the oven to 350°. Butter two 8-ounce ramekins and set them on a small baking sheet. In a small saucepan, melt the chocolate and butter over low heat, stirring occasionally. Let cool completely.

2. In a medium bowl, combine the egg, egg yolk, and granulated sugar. Set the bowl over a pan of simmering water and beat with a hand-held electric mixer at high speed until the mixture is thick and warm, about 4 minutes. Off the heat, continue beating the mixture until thick enough to form a slowly dissolving ribbon when the beater is lifted, about 2 minutes.

3. Fold the chocolate mixture into the egg mixture, then sift in the flour, gently folding it in. Divide the batter between the prepared ramekins and bake for about 20 minutes, or until well risen and set around the side but still soft in the center. Let cool for 2 minutes, then unmold each bombe onto a small plate. Sift the confectioners' sugar on top and serve.

—JONATHAN EISMANN

SCALLOP AND CHORIZO SAUTÉ

S auté comes from the French verb *sauter*, meaning to jump"
which is exactly what the scallops and chorizo slices do
when they hit the hot pan. This bold pairing of fresh seafood
and spicy sausage needs a side dish that is equally emphatic, hence
the roasted fennel with briny black olives in this menu. You will
want a loaf of warm crusty bread to soak up the flavorful juices. For
dessert, fresh fruit is recommended. Figs are in season through the
month of October.

A hearty Spanish red from Rioja, Navarra, or Ribera del
Duero will continue the Spanish theme of chorizo and
olives. For a French counterpoint, a northern Rhône Valley syrah,
like Cornas, St-Joseph, or a wonderful Hermitage will be perfect.

SCALLOPS AND SPICY CHORIZO

Spicy, garlicky chorizo is a pork sausage used in both Spanish and Mexican cooking. Spanish chorizo is made from smoked pork; the Mexican version uses fresh meat. Either type would be delicious in this recipe.

1½ teaspoons olive oil
  1 3-ounce chorizo sausage, quartered lengthwise and cut into
    ¼-inch-thick slices
 ½ pound sea scallops
    Salt and fresh-ground black pepper
  1 small leek, white and tender green parts only, quartered
    lengthwise, sliced into 2-by-¼-inch strips, and washed
 ¼ teaspoon minced garlic
2½ tablespoons dry white wine
 ¼ cup bottled clam juice

1. Heat ½ teaspoon of the oil in a large stainless-steel frying pan until almost smoking. Add the chorizo pieces and cook over high heat, stirring, until browned, about 2 minutes. Transfer to a plate. Wipe out the pan, add ½ teaspoon of the oil, and heat until almost smoking. Season the scallops with salt and pepper and add them to the pan. Cook over high heat, turning once, until golden, about 3 minutes. Add the scallops to the chorizo.

2. Heat the remaining ½ teaspoon oil in the frying pan. Add the leek and garlic and cook over moderately high heat, stirring, until just softened, about 2 minutes. Pour in the wine and boil until almost evaporated, scraping the bottom of the pan to loosen any brown bits. Pour in the clam juice and boil to reduce by half, about 2 minutes. Return the chorizo and scallops to the frying pan and toss over moderate heat until heated through. Serve at once.

—GRACE PARISI

SAUTÉING TIPS

• Have all your ingredients measured and close at hand. You will need to add them in quick succession to cook them evenly.
• Put the frying pan over moderate heat for a few minutes. Then add the oil and swirl it around until the palm of your hand feels hot when you hold it close above the pan.
• Never crowd the pan when sautéing. If the pan is too full, the temperature will drop and the food will not brown properly.
• When browning meat or seafood, be patient. If you constantly shake the pan and stir the contents, the food won't have a chance to brown.

GAME PLAN

Heat the oven.

Roast the fennel and soak the tomatoes.

Finish the fennel.

Cook the scallops and chorizo.

ROASTED FENNEL WITH OLIVES

Fennel is quite fibrous and needs a long cooking time to render it sweet and tender.

1 medium bulb fennel, trimmed and cut lengthwise
   into eighths
   Coarse salt and fresh-ground black pepper
4 sun-dried tomato halves (not oil-packed)
2 teaspoons butter
½ medium onion, sliced
¼ cup chicken stock or canned low-sodium chicken broth
6 Kalamata olives, pitted and quartered
1 tablespoon sliced fresh basil (optional)

1. Heat the oven to 450°. Place the fennel in an oiled baking dish, season with salt and pepper and roast for 20 minutes. Reduce the oven temperature to 375°.

2. Meanwhile, in a small bowl, cover the sun-dried tomatoes with hot water and let soak until softened, about 20 minutes. Drain and cut into slivers.

3. Melt the butter in a medium frying pan. Add the onion and cook over moderately high heat, stirring, until browned, about 5 minutes. Add the stock and bring to a simmer. Pour over the fennel, cover tightly with aluminum foil, and bake for 15 minutes. Uncover and bake for 20 minutes longer, or until the fennel is tender. Mix in the olives, sun-dried tomatoes, and basil, if using, and serve.

—BOB CHAMBERS

Winter

Italian-Style Steak with Basil
and Sage (p. 233) and Crisp Parmesan
Potatoes (p. 234)

Spaghetti with Garlic, Olive Oil, and
Tomato Paste (p. 267)

HOT SOUP FOR A COLD NIGHT

Hearty bean soups are usually too time-consuming for weeknight cooking, but a lentil soup is another matter. Unlike other dried legumes, lentils do not require soaking followed by hours of simmering. Tonight's warming soup with ham takes no more than forty-five minutes from start to finish. Corn bread spiked with spicy hot pepper and an escarole salad with a warm, garlicky vinaigrette are the piquant accompaniments. For dessert, serve tangerines or temple oranges.

Many red wines will complement this savory soup. On the leaner side, the herbaceousness of a French Chinon will play off the ham well. However, a fruitier wine, such as a zinfandel or merlot, will not overpower the meal.

LENTIL SOUP WITH HAM

If you can, use the tiny dark-green French Vertes du Puy lentils, which have a good flavor and hold their shape.

1 tablespoon olive oil
1 small onion, chopped
1 rib celery, cut into thin slices
1 carrot, cut into thin slices
1 clove garlic, minced
1 teaspoon dried thyme
1 bay leaf
2 tablespoons dry red wine
1 16-ounce can whole Italian plum tomatoes, drained and chopped
½ cup lentils, preferably Vertes du Puy, rinsed and picked over

3 cups chicken stock or canned low-sodium chicken broth
½ cup diced ham
   Salt and fresh-ground black pepper

1. In a large stainless-steel saucepan, heat the oil over moderate heat. Add the onion, celery, carrot, garlic, thyme, and bay leaf. Cover and cook until the onion is translucent, about 5 minutes.

2. Add the wine and bring to a simmer over high heat. Add the tomatoes, lentils, and stock and return to a boil. Reduce the heat to moderately low, cover partially, and simmer, stirring occasionally, until the lentils are tender, about 35 minutes. Add the ham and cook for 5 minutes. Remove the bay leaf, season the soup to taste with salt and pepper, and serve hot.

—STEPHANIE LYNESS

HOT-PEPPER CORN BREAD

Stone-ground cornmeal will give you the best flavor in a corn bread. It is more nutritious as well.

4 tablespoons unsalted butter
1 cup cornmeal
1 cup flour
2 tablespoons sugar
½ teaspoon salt
2 teaspoons baking powder
1 teaspoon dried red-pepper flakes
1 cup milk
2 eggs

1. Heat the oven to 425°. Place the butter in a 9- or 10-inch ovenproof frying pan, preferably cast iron, and heat in the oven until it has completely melted, about 2 minutes.

2. Meanwhile, in a medium bowl, whisk together the cornmeal, flour, sugar, salt, baking powder, and red-pepper flakes.

3. In a medium bowl, lightly whisk the milk with the eggs. Pour most of the melted butter into the egg mixture—leaving enough

GAME PLAN

Heat the oven.

Start the soup.

Mix and bake the corn bread.

Mix the salad dressing.

Finish the soup and toss the salad.

behind to generously coat the pan—and stir to combine.

4. Add the egg mixture to the dry ingredients and stir until just blended. Scrape the batter into the pan and smooth the surface with a spoon. Bake for 15 minutes, or until lightly golden. Let cool for a few minutes before serving directly from the pan.

—STEPHANIE LYNESS

WARM ESCAROLE SALAD

This is not meant to be a wilted salad, so use sturdy greens like escarole or chicory that will not lose their crunchiness when mixed with the warm vinaigrette.

½ head escarole or chicory (about ¾ pound),
   torn into 2-inch pieces
3 tablespoons olive oil
1 tablespoon wine vinegar
1½ teaspoons lemon juice
1 clove garlic, minced
   Salt and fresh-ground black pepper

Place the escarole in a salad bowl. In a small stainless-steel saucepan, combine the oil, vinegar, lemon juice, and garlic. Cook over moderate heat until hot, 2 to 3 minutes. Pour the dressing over the escarole and toss. Season with salt and pepper and serve immediately.

—STEPHANIE LYNESS

STEAK, ITALIAN STYLE

I t may come as a surprise that Tuscany's most famous dish is not a pasta or a stew, but a succulent and tender steak. *Bistecca alla fiorentina* is a large cut of *vitellone* (meat halfway between veal and beef) grilled over a wood fire and simply seasoned with a little olive oil. This menu looks to steak Florentine for inspiration and adds a few twists. Instead of using a whole steak, cut the beef into strips and pound it thin to tenderize the meat and help it to cook quickly. Then, along with the traditional drizzle of fine olive oil, toss fresh herbs into the pan for flavor. Serve panfried potatoes with Parmesan and a simple tomato and red onion salad alongside. And don't forget the bread to sop up the delicious pan juices. For dessert, the easily made rich chocolate mousse contains only three ingredients.

Indulging? The wonderful "super-Tuscan" style blends (usually sangiovese and cabernet) are not all as expensive as the famous Tignanello. Brusco dei Barbi is consistently a great value, and there are other full-bodied Tuscan reds to match as well.

ITALIAN-STYLE STEAK WITH BASIL AND SAGE
Double the recipe and use leftovers for steak-and-arugula sandwiches.

¾ pound boneless sirloin or strip steak, about 1 inch thick
 Salt and fresh-ground black pepper
1 small bunch arugula, stems removed
1 tablespoon balsamic vinegar
1 tablespoon olive oil
2 tablespoons thin-sliced fresh basil leaves
1½ tablespoons thin-sliced fresh sage leaves
1 tablespoon butter

233

1. Cut the sirloin on the diagonal against the grain into 12 even slices. Pound the steak slices between plastic wrap to a ¼-inch thickness. Generously season the meat on both sides with salt and pepper. Mound the arugula on two large plates and drizzle with the vinegar.

2. In a large heavy frying pan, heat the oil until almost smoking. Add the steak slices and cook over high heat until just browned, about 1½ minutes. Turn the meat, sprinkle with the basil and sage, and cook until browned and cooked to taste, about 1 more minute for very rare.

3. Add the butter to the frying pan and melt, scraping up any brown bits. Arrange the steak slices on the arugula, spoon the pan juices over the meat, and serve.

—JUDITH SUTTON

CRISP PARMESAN POTATOES
Patting the potato slices dry keeps them from sticking to the pan.

1   tablespoon cooking oil
2   medium Yukon Gold potatoes, scrubbed, cut into
     ¼-inch-thick slices, and patted dry
     Salt and fresh-ground black pepper
1½ tablespoons grated Parmesan

Heat the oil in a medium heavy frying pan. Add the potatoes, season with salt and pepper, and cook over moderately high heat, turning occasionally, until golden, 5 to 7 minutes. Reduce the heat to moderately low, cover partially, and cook, stirring occasionally, until the slices are lightly browned and tender, 10 to 12 minutes longer. Sprinkle the Parmesan over the potatoes and toss. Cover and cook until the cheese is melted, about 1 minute. Serve hot.

—JUDITH SUTTON

GAME PLAN

Make the mousse and refrigerate.

Slice the potatoes and cook until golden, and then lower the heat.

Make a simple salad with cherry tomatoes, red onion, and your favorite vinaigrette.

Cook the steak.

Add the cheese to the potatoes.

CHOCOLATE MOUSSE

*Italians would call this uncomplicated mousse a dolce al cucchiaio,
which roughly translates as dessert to be eaten with a spoon.*

2 ounces bittersweet chocolate, chopped
½ cup heavy cream
1 tablespoon Kahlúa or other coffee liqueur

1. In a medium metal bowl set over a pan of barely simmering water, melt the chocolate, stirring until smooth. Remove from the heat and let cool to tepid.

2. In a second medium bowl, whip the cream with the Kahlúa until soft peaks form. Stir about 2 tablespoons of the whipped cream into the melted chocolate, then fold in the remaining whipped cream; do not overwork or the mousse will be grainy. Spoon the mousse into two parfait glasses. Refrigerate the mousse until chilled, at least 30 minutes.

—JUDITH SUTTON

PECAN-COATED PORK CHOPS

I n this menu, which evokes the down-home flavors of the
South, marinated pork chops are coated with a crunchy mixture of cornmeal and chopped pecans and then panfried.
Steamed spinach, served on the side, gets a spoonful of tangy hot
sauce made with minced chile and two kinds of vinegar. Baked
sweet potatoes round out the main course. Store-bought gingersnaps, with a scoop of vanilla ice cream, are a sweet and spicy ending to this Dixie dinner.

Nuts, spice, and earthy sweet potatoes—a meal of such
warm, hearty flavors needs a wine of some complexity. The
grape is gewürztraminer. The region? Alsace, certainly, but a dry
version from Oregon will work well, too.

PECAN-COATED PORK CHOPS
*Pecans, like all nuts, contain a high percentage of oil. Shelled pecans can
quickly develop an off flavor if stored at room temperature; keep them in
the freezer and taste one or two before adding them to a recipe.*

¼ cup soy sauce
2 tablespoons lemon juice
1 tablespoon dark brown sugar
2 scallions including green tops, sliced thin
1 teaspoon bottled horseradish
2 center-cut pork chops (8 ounces each), about ¾ inch thick
2 tablespoons chopped pecans
2 tablespoons cornmeal
2 tablespoons flour
½ teaspoon salt

¼ teaspoon fresh-ground black pepper

2 tablespoons olive oil

1. In a small baking dish, combine the soy sauce, lemon juice, brown sugar, scallions, and horseradish. Add the pork chops, cover, and marinate for 30 minutes, turning occasionally.

2. In a sturdy paper bag, combine the pecans, cornmeal, flour, salt, and pepper. Put one of the pork chops in the bag and shake until well coated. Repeat with the remaining pork chop.

3. Heat the oil in a large heavy frying pan. Add the pork chops to the pan and cook over moderate heat until nicely browned and cooked through, 4 to 5 minutes per side. Transfer to warmed plates and serve at once.

—JESSICA B. HARRIS

STEAMED SPINACH WITH HOMEMADE HOT SAUCE

Use any leftover hot sauce to spice up cooked collard or mustard greens.

1 thyme sprig

2 tablespoons cider vinegar

1 tablespoon balsamic vinegar

1 tablespoon minced onion

1 tablespoon minced tomato

½ to 1 teaspoon minced jalapeño pepper

1 pound fresh spinach, stems removed, leaves washed
   Salt

1. In a small glass or stainless-steel bowl, combine all the ingredients except the spinach and salt. Cover the hot sauce and let stand for 30 minutes.

2. Heat a large heavy saucepan over high heat. Add the spinach in large handfuls, stirring to wilt it before adding another handful. When all the spinach has been added, cover and cook, stirring once or twice, until just tender, about 5 minutes. Drain the spinach well, season with salt, and serve with the hot sauce.

—JESSICA B. HARRIS

GAME PLAN

Heat the oven.

Pierce the sweet potatoes with a fork and bake.

Make the hot sauce for the spinach and the marinade for the pork chops.

Marinate the pork chops.

Cook the pork chops and the spinach.

PAPPARDELLE AND RATATOUILLE

Sunny Mediterranean flavors have a warming effect when it is cold outside. For tonight's main course, wide pasta is tossed with a boldly flavored olive paste containing lemon and orange zest, thyme, and red-pepper flakes. A winter ratatouille rounds out this satisfying meal. Dessert—a mug of hot spiced port and a biscotto or two—warrants a comfortable armchair and a toasty fire in the fireplace.

New Zealand sauvignon blancs are renowned for their exuberant aromas of grass and asparagus and their electrifying acidity. The bold vegetable flavors in the pappardelle and ratatouille require just this sort of intensity. Cloudy Bay is the most famous.

PAPPARDELLE WITH OLIVES, THYME, AND LEMON

16 black olives, such as Kalamata, pitted
2 tablespoons olive oil
   Zest of 1 lemon, chopped
1 3-inch strip orange zest, chopped
¼ teaspoon dried red-pepper flakes
½ cup flat-leaf parsley leaves
1 tablespoon minced fresh thyme
½ teaspoon coarse salt
½ pound pappardelle

1. In a mini-processor, combine the olives, oil, lemon and orange zests, red-pepper flakes, parsley, thyme, and salt. Pulse until chopped very fine but not pureed. Transfer the paste to a warm serving bowl.

2. In a large pot of boiling, salted water, cook the pappardelle until just done, about 12 minutes. Drain well, reserving ¼ cup of the pasta-cooking water.

3. Toss the pappardelle with the olive paste, adding some of the pasta-cooking water, 1 tablespoon at a time, if necessary. Serve immediately.

—JOHANNE KILLEEN AND GEORGE GERMON

QUICK WINTER RATATOUILLE

You will probably have leftovers with this recipe. Ratatouille will keep three to four days: Pour a thin film of olive oil over the top, cover with plastic wrap, and refrigerate.

- 3 tablespoons olive oil
- ½ onion, cut into thin slices
- 1 clove garlic, minced
- 1 small green bell pepper, sliced
- 1 baby zucchini, cut into ¼-inch-thick slices
- 1 small eggplant, halved lengthwise and cut into ½-inch-thick slices
- 1 16-ounce can whole Italian plum tomatoes, drained and chopped
- 1 teaspoon minced flat-leaf parsley
- ¼ teaspoon dried winter savory
- ¼ teaspoon dried marjoram
- ½ teaspoon fresh-ground black pepper
- ¼ teaspoon salt
- 2 tablespoons pine nuts

1. In a large stainless-steel frying pan, heat 1 tablespoon of the oil over moderate heat. Add the onion and cook, stirring occasionally, until softened, about 4 minutes. Add the garlic and bell pepper and cook 2 minutes more. Increase the heat to high, add the zucchini, and cook, stirring, until the vegetables begin to brown, about 5 minutes. Transfer the vegetables to a medium bowl and reserve.

2. Add the remaining 2 tablespoons of oil to the pan. Heat the oil until very hot. Add the eggplant and cook until softened and

GAME PLAN

Prepare the ratatouille.

Put a pot of water on to boil for the pasta.

Prepare the olive paste for the pasta.

Cook the pasta, drain it, and toss with the olive paste.

Warm the spiced port just before serving.

browned, 5 to 7 minutes. Stir in the tomatoes, parsley, winter savory, marjoram, and the reserved vegetables. Reduce the heat to moderate and let the mixture simmer until thick, about 5 minutes. Add the pepper and salt. Let cool to room temperature.

3. Just before serving, toast the pine nuts in a small dry pan over moderate heat until lightly browned. Shake the pan often to prevent scorching. Sprinkle the ratatouille with the warm pine nuts and serve.

—ANNE WALSH

HOT SPICED PORT

Don't pour your best vintage port into the saucepan for this recipe. Moderately priced ruby or tawny ports are perfectly fine.

   1 teaspoon sugar
   2 teaspoons water
1½ cups port
     Pinch ground cloves
     Pinch ground allspice
     Pinch grated nutmeg
   2 strips lemon zest

In a medium stainless-steel saucepan, dissolve the sugar in the water over moderate heat. Add the port, cloves, and allspice. Warm through, about 5 minutes. Pour into mugs and top each with a pinch of nutmeg and a strip of lemon zest.

—ANNE WALSH

PANFRIED DUO

Whether it is bacon and eggs or meat and potatoes, you could say that some foods are just made for each other. That is certainly the case with quail and cornmeal—in northern Italy and the American South, quail is frequently served with polenta (as it is known in Italy) or grits (as we call it here). Comforting polenta has an affinity for many savory meats, and in this menu it works nicely with both quail and mild Italian sausages. Baked onions and steamed Brussels sprouts complete the main course. A very light dessert is in order after such robust fare; we suggest juicy, sweet clementines, which abound at this time of year.

Wines from the Rhône valley will have the body to stand up to the flavors of this great winter meal. A Châteauneuf-du-Pape would work, or for pure Syrah fruit, travel north and look for a wine from Cornas.

PANFRIED QUAIL AND ITALIAN SAUSAGE
Quail are farm-raised and readily available. They need only ten minutes to cook and never fail to impress.

2 links mild Italian sausage
1 cup water
2 quail
¼ teaspoon salt
½ teaspoon herbes de Provence
1 tablespoon butter
1 teaspoon olive oil

1. Prick the sausages all over with a fork. In a large heavy frying pan, heat the sausages and water. Cook over high heat, turning the sausages once or twice, until the water evaporates, about 5 minutes. Reduce the heat to moderate and cook, turning occasionally, until browned, about 12 minutes longer.

2. Meanwhile, put a quail, breast-side down, on a work surface. Use poultry shears to cut along both sides of the back bone and remove it. Turn the quail over and press firmly on the breast bone to break the bone and flatten the bird slightly. Repeat the procedure with the other quail. Rub the birds all over with the salt and herbes de Provence.

3. When the sausages are browned, push them to one side of the pan. Wipe out excess grease with a paper towel. Add the butter and oil to the pan. When quite hot, add the quail, skin-side down. Cook until well browned, about 5 minutes. Turn and cook until browned on the other side, about 5 minutes. Place a quail and a sausage on each of two warm dinner plates and serve.

—ANNE WALSH

POLENTA

½ cup cornmeal
2 cups water
½ teaspoon salt
1 bay leaf
1 tablespoon butter
¼ cup grated Parmesan

1. In a small bowl, combine the cornmeal with ½ cup of cold water. Mix until blended.

2. In a heavy small saucepan, combine the remaining 1½ cups of water, the salt, and bay leaf and bring to a boil over high heat. With a wooden spoon, stir in the cornmeal paste and return to a boil, stirring constantly. Reduce the heat to low and continue cooking, stirring occasionally, until the polenta has thickened, 10 to 12 minutes. Remove and discard the bay leaf.

GAME PLAN

Heat the oven and bake the onions.

Panfry the sausages.

Cook the polenta.

Season and panfry the quail.

243

Add the butter and stir until incorporated. Cover the polenta to keep warm until ready to serve.

3. Divide the polenta between the dinner plates. Sprinkle the Parmesan on top just before serving.

—ANNE WALSH

BAKED SLICED ONIONS

1 medium onion, cut into 4 slices
¼ teaspoon salt
Pinch dried sage
2 teaspoons butter

Heat the oven to 350°. Place the onion slices in a small buttered baking dish. Season with the salt and sage. Dot with the butter. Bake for 40 minutes, or until soft.

—ANNE WALSH

INSTANT SOUP

The secret to serving delicious soup in minutes has nothing to do with getting out the can opener. Powerful ingredients that add flavor quickly are the key when time is short. In our creamy corn chowder, smoked trout provides the needed depth and richness. You will want to serve toasted rolls along with the soup and a salad of peppery greens, such as watercress, arugula, or radicchio. There is an old-fashioned butterscotch pudding for dessert: Although it is not instant, the pudding is well worth the fifteen minutes work.

Chardonnays from Mâcon rarely reach the dizzying heights (in complexity *or* price) of white Burgundies like Montrachet, but have character nonetheless. Enjoy the creamy texture and apple-like flavors of a Saint-Véran or Mâcon-Prissé.

SMOKED TROUT CHOWDER
Smoked shrimp or smoked mussels make fine substitutes for the trout.

1½ tablespoons butter
1 small onion, minced
1 rib celery, sliced thin
2 small red potatoes, cut into ¾-inch chunks
Pinch dried thyme
1 cup bottled clam juice
1½ cups hot water
4 ounces smoked trout fillet, skinned and flaked
½ cup fresh (cut from 1 ear) or frozen corn kernels
½ cup heavy cream
1 tablespoon minced flat-leaf parsley
Salt and fresh-ground black pepper

1. In a large heavy saucepan, melt the butter over moderately high heat. Add the onion and celery and stir for about 5 minutes. Add the potatoes and thyme and cook until just heated through, about 1 minute. Add the clam juice and the hot water and bring to a boil.

2. Reduce the heat to moderately low, cover, and cook until the potatoes are just tender, about 7 minutes. Add the trout, corn, and cream. Cover and cook over low heat until the vegetables are tender, about 5 minutes. Add the parsley, season with salt and pepper, and serve.

—GRACE PARISI

QUICK SOUP TIPS
• Check out supermarket or health-food market salad bars for ready-to-use ingredients, such as precut vegetables and cooked shrimp, chicken, and meats.
• Use frozen vegetables, such as corn, peas, or spinach, to cut prep time.
• Give bottled clam juice extra flavor by simmering reserved shrimp shells or fish bones and some chopped onion in the juice for ten minutes; strain the liquid and use for seafood soups.

BUTTERSCOTCH PUDDING

This recipe makes a rich, creamy, and not-too-sweet pudding with a wallop of butterscotch flavor.

4 large egg yolks
⅔ cup heavy cream
¼ cup dark brown sugar
2 tablespoons unsalted butter, cut into pieces
3 tablespoons milk
¼ teaspoon vanilla extract

GAME PLAN

Cook and chill the puddings.

Prepare salad greens and make a mustardy vinaigrette.

Make the soup.

Split, butter, and broil the rolls.

1. In the top of a double boiler, lightly whisk the egg yolks. In a small saucepan, warm the cream over moderate heat until steaming; keep hot.

2. In a small heavy frying pan, cook the brown sugar and butter over moderately high heat, stirring with a wooden spoon, until melted and bubbling, about 2 minutes. Remove from the heat and stir in the hot cream until blended. Let cool for 2 minutes, then stir in the milk.

3. Gently whisk the butterscotch mixture into the egg yolks. Stir in the vanilla. Set the pan over simmering water and cook over moderate heat, stirring, until the pudding thickens slightly and reaches 165° to 170°, about 6 minutes. Do not overcook.

4. Strain into a heatproof bowl and stir for 2 minutes to prevent a skin from forming. Transfer to two 6-ounce ramekins and let cool to room temperature. Cover and refrigerate for at least 1 hour or up to 2 days.

—SHELLEY BORIS

TURKEY SCHNITZEL AND CHIPS

Turkey cutlets are an economical and readily available alternative to veal for an easy dinner. For this Austrian-style recipe, the cutlets are coated with egg white and mustard, and breaded to keep them moist; they are then panfried. Oven-crisped potato slices and a zesty salad of broccoli, orange, and roasted peppers complete the hearty meal. For dessert, pick up a pumpkin pie from your favorite bakery.

A judiciously oaked Californian or Australian chardonnay is a perfect match for this dinner. Even if you favor big oaky whites, you may find they dull the delicate flavor of the turkey.

TURKEY SCHNITZEL

Schnitzel *is simply the German word for cutlet. Wiener Schnitzel, so popular in Austria, is a veal cutlet dipped in egg, breaded, and fried. Here we use turkey and get much the same effect.*

- 1 egg white
- ½ teaspoon water
- 1 tablespoon Dijon mustard
- ¾ teaspoon salt
- ½ cup dry bread crumbs
- ¼ teaspoon fresh-ground black pepper
- ½ pound turkey cutlets, sliced about ¼ inch thick
- 3 tablespoons olive oil
  Lemon wedges, for serving

1. In a medium bowl, beat the egg white and water until frothy. Mix in the mustard and ¼ teaspoon of the salt. On a plate, mix the

bread crumbs with the remaining ½ teaspoon salt and the pepper.

2. Dip each cutlet in the egg-white mixture and then coat both sides with the seasoned bread crumbs. Place the cutlets on a platter and refrigerate for about 30 minutes.

3. In a large frying pan, heat the oil over high heat until very hot. Add the cutlets and cook, turning once, until golden brown and cooked through, 1 to 2 minutes per side. Transfer to paper towels to drain. Serve with lemon wedges.

—SUSAN SHAPIRO JASLOVE

OVEN-TOASTED POTATO CHIPS
Use the slicing blade of a food processor to cut uniform potato slices.

½ pound new potatoes, sliced a generous ⅛ inch thick
1 tablespoon olive oil
¼ teaspoon salt

1. Heat the oven to 500°. In a colander, rinse the sliced potatoes under cold water; pat dry. Toss the potatoes with the oil and ⅛ teaspoon of the salt and spread them on a large baking sheet in a single layer.

2. Toast the potatoes on the top rack of the oven, rotating the baking sheet, for 20 to 25 minutes, or until golden brown. Drain on paper towels and sprinkle with the remaining ⅛ teaspoon salt. Serve warm.

—SUSAN SHAPIRO JASLOVE

BROCCOLI, ORANGE, AND ROASTED-PEPPER SALAD
Roasted red bell peppers in a jar are a great convenience food; keep them on hand for last-minute suppers.

1½ cups broccoli florets
1 medium orange
1 to 2 roasted red bell peppers from a jar, rinsed and
cut into thin strips
1 tablespoon wine vinegar

GAME PLAN

Heat the oven.

Coat the turkey cutlets and refrigerate.

Prepare the potato chips.

Make the salad.

Fry the cutlets.

1½ teaspoons olive oil
⅛ teaspoon cayenne
⅛ teaspoon salt

1. Steam the broccoli florets in a steamer basket over simmering water until just tender, about 7 minutes. Rinse with cold water and drain well. Set aside in a large bowl.

2. Slice off the top and bottom of the orange. Stand the orange upright on a work surface. Using a small sharp knife, cut away the skin and white pith. Cut between the membranes to release the sections and add them to the broccoli. Mix in the roasted-pepper strips.

3. Just before serving, add the vinegar and oil and toss to combine. Season with the cayenne and salt.

—SUSAN SHAPIRO JASLOVE

CHICKEN AND DUMPLINGS FOR DINNER

A hearty serving of chicken-and-dumplings just like Mom used to make (or wished she could) will help take the chill out of a winter's night. If you like, serve the stew with a green salad, such as red leaf or Bibb lettuce, tossed with a buttermilk dressing. At the end of the meal, treat yourself and your partner to oatmeal chocolate-chip cookies.

There is nothing complicated about this comforting dish, so why complicate the wine? A *dry* chenin blanc from California makes a delicious pairing with this stew. Chappellet is the label to find.

CHICKEN STEW WITH CORNMEAL DUMPLINGS

Canned chicken broth will make a perfectly acceptable stew, but if you have the time, make your own chicken stock using the recipe on the following page. You can freeze the extra for countless other uses.

1 pound chicken pieces
3 cups Chicken Stock, page 254, or canned low-sodium
   chicken broth
1 bay leaf
1 medium celery rib, sliced crosswise
2 medium carrots, peeled and sliced on the diagonal
   into 1-inch-thick pieces
4 small white onions, halved lengthwise
2 large sprigs of fresh thyme
1 cup packed coarse-chopped kale leaves
   Salt and fresh-ground black pepper

CORNMEAL DUMPLINGS

½ cup flour
¼ cup cornmeal
1 teaspoon baking powder
¼ teaspoon salt
1 tablespoon cold unsalted butter, cut into pieces
⅓ cup milk

1. *Prepare the stew:* In a large saucepan, combine the chicken pieces, stock, and bay leaf and bring to a boil over high heat. Re-

GAME PLAN

If using, make homemade chicken stock.

Heat the oven.

Mix and bake the bars.

Prepare the stew.

Make and poach the dumplings.

Assemble a simple salad.

CHICKEN STOCK

Canned chicken broth is a great convenience, but it cannot quite match the flavor of homemade stock. Make this recipe if you have the time and keep the extra on hand for use in soups, sautés, and sauces. Often, recipes for two call for just a tablespoon or two of stock; we suggest first freezing stock in ice-cube trays and then storing the cubes in a resealable plastic container.

5¼ pounds chicken carcasses, backs, wings, and/or necks, plus gizzards (optional)
3 onions, quartered
3 carrots, quartered
3 ribs celery, quartered
10 parsley stems
6 peppercorns
2½ quarts water

Put all the ingredients in a large pot. Bring to a boil and skim the foam that rises to the surface. Reduce the heat and simmer, partially covered, for 2 hours. Strain. Press the bones and vegetables firmly to get all the liquid. Skim the fat from the surface if using immediately. If not, the stock can be refrigerated for up to a week or frozen. Remove the fat from the surface before using. Makes about 2 quarts.

duce the heat to moderate, turn the chicken over, cover, and simmer for 10 minutes.

2. Skim the broth of any fat. Stir in the celery, carrots, onions, and thyme sprigs. Continue to simmer over moderate heat, partially covered, until the carrots and onions are just tender, about 15 minutes. Stir in the kale. Season to taste with salt and pepper.

3. *Prepare the dumplings:* In a medium bowl, whisk together the flour, cornmeal, baking powder, and salt. With your fingertips, work the butter into the flour until the mixture is crumbly. Using a fork, stir in the milk until blended.

4. Drop tablespoons of the dumpling batter in 8 clumps over the top of the stew. Reduce the heat to moderately low, cover, and simmer until the dumplings are cooked through, about 10 minutes. Discard the bay leaf and thyme sprigs and serve the stew immediately in shallow soup bowls.

—Susan Shapiro Jaslove

OATMEAL CHOCOLATE-CHIP BARS
The chewy bars will keep for up to a week in a cookie tin.

¼ pound cold unsalted butter, cut into pieces
½ cup light brown sugar
1 egg
½ teaspoon vanilla extract
½ cup flour
½ teaspoon baking soda
¼ teaspoon salt
1½ cups old-fashioned rolled oats
1 package (6 ounces) semisweet chocolate chips

1. Heat the oven to 375°. Butter an 8-inch square baking pan and set aside.

2. In a food processor, process the butter and brown sugar until light and fluffy, scraping down the bowl occasionally. Add the egg and vanilla and process until just combined.

3. In a medium bowl, whisk together the flour, baking soda, and salt. Add the dry mixture to the processor and process, scraping down the bowl once, until blended. Transfer the batter to the medium bowl. Stir in the oats and chocolate chips.

4. Scrape the batter into the prepared pan and spread evenly. Bake until set and golden brown, 20 to 25 minutes. Cut into 12 bars while still slightly warm. Remove from the pan and serve at once or set aside on a rack to cool.

—Susan Shapiro Jaslove

FRENCH COUNTRY FAVORITES

Thick-cut lamb loin chops are a tried-and-true, delicious main dish, here embellished with a red-wine sauce. The creamy potato gratin gets extra flavor from chicken stock. Sautéed Swiss chard makes an ideal additional side dish.

Dessert is as classic as the lamb chops, though perhaps less familiar. A traditional French country *clafouti* consists of black cherries baked under a layer of thick pancake batter, but these days the fruit can vary with the season, and a *clafouti* can be dense and eggy or light and dry like ours.

In Cahors, south of Bordeaux, hearty wines based on the unusual tannat grape variety are made—sort of country versions of Bordeaux. Château Lagrezette is probably the most widely available example of this full, flavorful, firmly structured red.

LAMB CHOPS WITH RED WINE AND THYME
The technique is classic—sauté the meat, deglaze the pan with a little wine, and swirl in butter to finish—and there is no reason to do anything more elaborate than this for superb lamb.

    1   tablespoon cooking oil
    4   lamb loin chops, about 1¼ to 1½ inches thick
        Salt and fresh-ground black pepper
    3   tablespoons red wine
    ½   teaspoon chopped fresh thyme
    1½ teaspoons butter

1. Heat a large stainless-steel frying pan over moderately high heat for 5 minutes. Add the oil. Season the lamb chops on both

sides with salt and pepper, add them to the pan and cook, turning once, until lightly browned, about 3 minutes per side. Reduce the heat to moderate and cook until done to taste, 2 minutes longer on each side for medium rare.

2. Transfer the lamb chops to a warmed platter and cover loosely with aluminum foil. Pour off the fat from the pan, add the wine, and scrape the bottom of the pan to loosen the brown bits. Stir in the thyme. Cook the sauce until thickened, about 1 minute. Pour in any accumulated lamb juices. Remove the pan from the heat and swirl in the butter. Pour the sauce over the chops.

—STEPHANIE LYNESS

POTATO GRATIN

   2   baking potatoes, peeled
   1   clove garlic, minced
       Salt and fresh-ground black pepper
   ¾   cup chicken stock or canned low-sodium chicken broth
   ¼   cup heavy cream
1½   teaspoons butter, at room temperature

1. Heat the oven to 375°. Butter a 1-quart gratin or shallow baking dish. In a food processor fitted with a medium slicing disk or using a large knife, slice the potatoes crosswise about ⅛ inch thick.

2. Arrange half of the potato slices, overlapping, in the bottom of the prepared dish. Sprinkle the potatoes with the garlic. Season generously with salt and pepper. Top with the remaining potatoes, and season with salt and pepper. Pour in the stock and cream. Dot with the butter.

3. Bake the gratin for 35 to 40 minutes, until the potatoes are tender and the top is brown. Let cool for 10 to 15 minutes before serving.

—STEPHANIE LYNESS

GAME PLAN

Heat the oven.

Assemble the potato gratin and bake.

Prepare and bake the *clafoutis.*

Rinse and chop the Swiss chard.

Cook the lamb chops.

Sauté the chard in olive oil.

INDIVIDUAL PRUNE CLAFOUTIS

Because these prune clafoutis contain so little flour, they bake like soufflés, and will fall as they cool.

2 teaspoons plus ¼ cup sugar
¾ cup pitted prunes
1 large egg
1 large egg yolk
1 teaspoon vanilla extract
2 tablespoons flour
½ cup milk
½ cup heavy cream

1. Heat the oven to 375°. Butter two 5-inch gratin or shallow baking dishes. Sprinkle 1 teaspoon of the sugar inside each dish and tilt to coat. Scatter the prunes on top.

2. In a medium bowl, whisk together the egg, egg yolk, vanilla, and the remaining ¼ cup sugar until smooth. Add the flour and whisk briefly. Add the milk and cream and whisk until incorporated. Pour the mixture into the prepared dishes and bake for about 25 minutes, until puffed and browned. Set aside to cool for at least 10 minutes before serving.

—Stephanie Lyness

STRATA'S HERE

S avory strata—the cheese, bread, and egg dish most often seen on brunch tables—makes a satisfying main course for a casual dinner. Serve it with a watercress salad and the Italian bread left over from preparing the strata. To end the meal, a very common fruit is transformed into a most uncommon topping for vanilla ice cream: Sweet, crunchy banana brittle is fun to make and even more fun to eat.

Eggs and tannin just don't get along, so the best route for this meal is a white wine. A chardonnay from Australia, California, or even Chile will have the body to match the richness of the ham and cheese.

HAM-AND-CHEESE STRATA
For this rich, tasty main dish, soak the bread in the egg mixture while you cut up the other ingredients.

  4 large eggs
¾ cup milk
¼ teaspoon salt
¼ teaspoon fresh-ground black pepper
  2 cups 1-inch cubes of Italian bread
  3 ounces country ham, such as Smithfield,
     cut into ½-inch dice (¾ cup)
  3 ounces Gouda, cut into ¾-inch dice (¾ cup)
¼ cup sun-dried tomatoes packed in oil, drained, and
     cut into slivers
  3 tablespoons minced fresh chives
½ cup grated cheddar

1. Heat the oven to 425°. In a large bowl, whisk together the eggs, milk, salt, and pepper. Stir in the bread; let soak. Add the ham, Gouda, tomatoes, and 2 tablespoons of the chives to the egg mixture and stir.

2. Butter a shallow 1-quart baking dish; pour in the mixture. Sprinkle the cheddar on top. Bake for 15 to 20 minutes, or until puffed and golden. Let cool slightly, sprinkle with the remaining chives, and serve.

—DIANA STURGIS

DUTCH TREAT

Authentic Gouda (pronounced "khowda" in Dutch) from Holland is dotted with tiny holes and has a mellow, nutty flavor. When aged a year or longer, the cheese develops a complexity much like a fine sharp cheddar and sometimes crunchy granules like those found in good Parmesan. American Goudas are rarely aged and tend to be very bland. If you cannot find a good imported Gouda, substitute Edam or a sharp cheddar.

GAME PLAN

Heat the oven to 425°.

Prepare and bake the strata.

Wash the watercress and refrigerate. Make the dressing.

Prepare the banana brittle; bake it at 350° after the strata is done.

Toss the salad.

WATERCRESS SALAD

2 teaspoons lemon juice
2 tablespoons olive oil
  Salt and fresh-ground black pepper
1 small bunch watercress, tough stems removed

In a bowl, whisk together the lemon juice, oil, and salt and pepper to taste. Just before serving, whisk the dressing again, add the watercress and toss.

—DIANA STURGIS

BANANA BRITTLE

The brittle can be wrapped in waxed paper and kept in an airtight container for up to five days.

- 1 tablespoon unsalted butter
- 1 teaspoon cooking oil
- 2 tablespoons sugar
- 1 semiripe large banana, cut into very thin slices
- ¼ teaspoon cinnamon
- 2 tablespoons chopped unsalted peanuts

1. Heat the oven to 350°. On a rimmed baking sheet, melt the butter with the oil. Spread to coat the pan evenly and sprinkle with 1 tablespoon of the sugar. Cover with the banana slices in a slightly overlapping layer. Sprinkle with the remaining 1 tablespoon sugar, the cinnamon, and peanuts.

2. Bake the banana slices for about 20 minutes, or until the slices around the edge are crisp and golden. Let cool slightly so they firm up. Transfer the browned slices to a plate and bake the rest for about 3 minutes longer, or until browned.

—MARCIA KIESEL

PAN-SEARED SALMON

Pan-searing is one of the easiest ways to prepare salmon. Just heat up the pan, add the fish, and in a matter of minutes the fillets have a crisp, golden crust. Tabbouleh, the Middle Eastern bulgur-herb salad, provides a refreshing contrast to the rich salmon, as do tender sautéed cucumber slices. For dessert, you can whip up impressive coconut chocolate ice-cream tarts from only three ingredients. The salmon should be seared at the last minute, but the rest of the meal can be made in advance.

Try this salmon with a pinot noir tonight. Lighter, spicier styles from Oregon and France will make the best pairing, but even the more powerful examples won't overwhelm the salmon's deep flavors and meaty consistency.

CRISP PAN-SEARED SALMON

Perfect pan-seared salmon depends on a very hot pan. Use a heavy cast-iron skillet or frying pan that heats evenly. Warm the pan before you add the oil; this restaurant trick allows the pan to get really hot without burning the oil. A preheated pan also requires less oil. Try this method with other meaty fish or even with sea scallops; they will be golden brown outside and tender inside.

½ teaspoon olive oil
12 ounces skinless center-cut salmon fillet, about 1¼ inches thick, cut into 2 pieces
¼ teaspoon coarse salt
Fresh-ground black pepper

Set a cast-iron frying pan over high heat. When a drop of water skitters on the surface, after about 3 minutes, add the oil. Tilt the pan to coat the bottom evenly and heat until the oil is almost smoking, about 30 seconds. Season the salmon with the salt and pepper. Add the salmon to the pan, skinned-side up, and cook until golden brown on the bottom, about 4 minutes. Turn the salmon, lower the heat to moderate, and sear until just cooked, 3 to 4 minutes longer.

—JUDITH SUTTON

TABBOULEH

If you prefer it or just want a change, whole-wheat instant couscous is a good substitute for bulgur in tabbouleh.

½ cup bulgur, rinsed
½ cup minced flat-leaf parsley
3 tablespoons chopped fresh mint leaves
4 scallions including green tops, sliced thin
2 tablespoons olive oil
1 tablespoon lemon juice
   Salt and fresh-ground black pepper
   Generous dash cayenne

1. Put the bulgur in a medium bowl and add hot water to cover by 2 inches. Let soak for 15 minutes. Drain the bulgur in a fine strainer, pressing on the grains to extract excess water. Transfer to a bowl.

2. Add the parsley, mint, scallions, oil, and lemon juice and toss. Season with salt, black pepper, and cayenne and toss. Cover and let stand for at least 20 minutes.

—JUDITH SUTTON

GAME PLAN

Heat the oven and toast the coconut.

Assemble the ice-cream tartlets.

Make the tabbouleh.

Cook the cucumbers.

Sear the salmon.

GLAZED CUCUMBERS

  1 medium cucumber, peeled, halved lengthwise, and seeded
1½ teaspoons butter
    Salt and fresh-ground black pepper

Slice the cucumber on the diagonal into ¼-inch-thick slices. Melt the butter in a large frying pan. Add the cucumbers, season with salt and pepper, and cook over moderately high heat, stirring occasionally, until tender, 5 to 7 minutes.

—JUDITH SUTTON

CHOCOLATE COCONUT ICE-CREAM TARTLETS

The tartlets can be made well in advance and kept frozen for two or three days.

  6 tablespoons shredded sweetened coconut
  1 tablespoon unsalted butter, melted
 ½ pint chocolate ice cream, slightly softened

1. Heat the oven to 375°. Toast the coconut on a baking sheet for 8 to 10 minutes, stirring occasionally, until golden. Transfer the toasted coconut to a bowl and let cool slightly. Add the butter and stir until incorporated. Pat the mixture into two 3-inch tartlet molds. Freeze until firm, about 10 minutes.

2. Spoon the ice cream into the two coconut shells, mounding it slightly in the center and spreading it out to the edge of the shells; be careful not to dislodge any of the coconut. Cover and freeze for at least 30 minutes, or until ready to serve.

—JUDITH SUTTON

PURE-AND-SIMPLE PASTA

I f it's too late to run to the store and the refrigerator is next to empty, don't worry; you won't have to call for a pizza delivery. The not-so-glamorous ingredients for the spaghetti (garlic, olive oil, tomato paste, some herbs) are sure to be in your kitchen. A speedily assembled sauce delivers pure, intense flavor. Make the salad with romaine lettuce, a good green to have on hand because it stays fresh for several days in the refrigerator's crisper bin. Baked pears make a very Italian, and truly effortless, dessert.

Chianti is the all-too-easy pairing, but there are a number of sangiovese-based wines that will expand your horizon and pair well with this simple, robust pasta. Try a Vino Nobile di Montepulciano or Lungarotti's Rubesco.

SPAGHETTI WITH GARLIC, OLIVE OIL, AND TOMATO PASTE

Use your best olive oil for this recipe and serve the spaghetti the moment it is done—that's when it is at its best. To keep it steaming, heat your serving bowls; thick china will hold the heat best.

- ½ pound spaghetti or spaghettini
- ¼ cup olive oil
- 2 tablespoons tomato paste
- 1½ teaspoons minced garlic
- 1 teaspoon coarse salt
- 2 tablespoons chopped flat-leaf parsley
- 1 tablespoon shredded fresh basil
  Julienned scallions, for garnish (optional)

1. In a large pot of boiling, salted water, cook the spaghetti until just done, about 9 minutes.

2. Meanwhile, in a stainless-steel frying pan large enough to hold the pasta, combine the oil, tomato paste, garlic, and salt. Cook over moderately low heat, stirring occasionally, until the garlic is golden, about 5 minutes. Remove from the heat.

3. Drain the spaghetti, add it to the pan and toss well. Add the parsley and basil and toss again. Transfer to plates, top with the scallions, if using, and serve immediately.

—JOHANNE KILLEEN AND GEORGE GERMON

ROMAINE-AND-TOASTED-WALNUT SALAD

2 tablespoons chopped walnuts
2 teaspoons sherry vinegar
  Salt and fresh-ground black pepper
1½ tablespoons olive oil
2 teaspoons walnut oil
1 small head romaine lettuce, torn into 2-inch pieces

1. Heat the oven to 400°. Spread the walnuts on a baking sheet and toast for about 5 minutes, or until fragrant.

2. In a bowl, whisk the vinegar with a pinch each of salt and pepper. Whisk in the olive and walnut oils. Add the romaine and toss to coat. Sprinkle with the toasted walnuts and serve.

—STEPHANIE LYNESS

BAKED PEARS WITH GINGER

1 tablespoon unsalted butter
1 teaspoon minced fresh ginger
2 Comice or other winter pears
2 tablespoons sugar
2 tablespoons dry white wine
  Plain yogurt or sour cream

GAME PLAN

Heat the oven.

Put a pot of water on to boil for the pasta.

Toast the walnuts for the salad; bake the pears.

Make the salad.

Cook the pasta and its sauce.

1. Heat the oven to 400°. Smear the bottom of a small baking dish with half the butter; sprinkle the ginger on top.

2. Peel, halve, and core the pears. Place them cut-side down in a single layer in the prepared pan. Sprinkle the sugar on top, pour the wine over the pears, and dot with the remaining butter. Cover tightly with aluminum foil and bake for about 30 minutes, until the pears are tender (the time will vary depending on their ripeness). Let cool slightly.

3. Place the pears on two dessert plates and spoon the juices over the pears. Serve warm or at room temperature with a dollop of yogurt or sour cream.

—STEPHANIE LYNESS

FIVE-MINUTE CHICKEN

The great French chef Auguste Escoffier had two words that ought to be the motto for weeknight cooks everywhere: *"Faites simple."* The centerpiece of tonight's menu could hardly be more simple: The pounded chicken breasts cook in three minutes (really), and the sauce is ready in two. Kugel, a warming baked-noodle casserole, and chicory salad round out the meal. For dessert, serve sliced navel oranges sprinkled with some pomegranate seeds.

The fruity impression of an Alsace pinot gris (or Tokay Pinot Gris)—with a dry, complex finish—will play off the mustard in this dish, yet the flavors are delicate enough for chicken.

SAUTÉED CHICKEN BREASTS WITH MUSTARD SAUCE
The four-ingredient mustard sauce is equally delicious over fish or veal or turkey cutlets.

  2 boneless, skinless chicken breasts (about 5 ounces each)
      Salt and fresh-ground black pepper
1½ teaspoons olive oil
½ cup dry white wine
  2 teaspoons lemon juice
1½ teaspoons Dijon mustard
  4 teaspoons butter, cut into small pieces

1. Pound each chicken breast between sheets of waxed paper until flattened to about ¼ inch. Season with salt and pepper.

2. In a large, heavy, stainless-steel frying pan, heat the oil. Add the breasts and sauté over moderately high heat until golden

brown and just cooked through, about 1½ minutes per side. Transfer to a platter and keep warm.

3. Add the wine and lemon juice to the pan and cook over high heat, scraping up any brown bits, until the liquid is reduced by half, about 2 minutes. Whisk in the mustard. Remove the pan from the heat and whisk in the butter, a few pieces at a time. Add any accumulated juices from the chicken to the sauce and season with salt and pepper. Spoon the sauce over the chicken and serve hot.

—SUSAN SHAPIRO JASLOVE

KUGEL WITH CARAMELIZED ONIONS

A traditional favorite among Jewish families, kugel can be either a sweet or savory dish. Here, the caramelized onions and the raisins lend a hint of sweetness.

1 tablespoon butter
1 teaspoon olive oil
2 medium onions, cut into thin slices
6 ounces wide egg noodles
1 large egg, beaten to mix
2 tablespoons raisins
  Salt and fresh-ground black pepper

GAME PLAN

Heat the oven.

Prepare and bake the kugel.

Toast the walnuts for the salad.

Make the salad dressing and wash the chicory.

Sauté the chicken breasts and make the sauce.

Toss the salad.

1. Heat the oven to 425°. Butter an 8-inch pie plate.

2. In a medium heavy frying pan, melt the butter with the oil until foamy. Add the onions and cook over moderately high heat, stirring frequently, until golden brown, about 15 minutes.

3. In a large pot of boiling, salted water, cook the noodles until almost tender but still slightly underdone, about 8 minutes. Drain. Wipe out the pot, return the noodles to it, and stir in the onions. Add the egg, raisins, salt, and pepper and toss gently.

4. Transfer the noodle mixture to the prepared pie plate and bake for about 25 minutes, or until set and golden brown. Cut into wedges and serve.

—SUSAN SHAPIRO JASLOVE

CHICORY SALAD

The bitter chicory balances the faint sweetness of the kugel.

¼ cup walnut pieces, chopped
1 tablespoon wine vinegar
2 tablespoons olive oil
  Salt and fresh-ground black pepper
½ medium head chicory, torn into 2-inch pieces

1. Heat the oven to 425°. Spread the walnuts in a pie plate and toast for 5 minutes, or until fragrant.

2. In a small glass or stainless-steel bowl, whisk together the vinegar and oil and season with salt and pepper. Just before serving, toss the dressing with the chicory and sprinkle with the toasted walnuts.

—SUSAN SHAPIRO JASLOVE

STEAK AND POTATOES

Hungry for a straightforward meal full of good, honest flavor? A juicy piece of beef and a mound of buttery mashed potatoes cannot be beat. For a dinner for two, New York strip steaks have many advantages; they are tender and flavorful, and one steak is just the right size for one person. An unadorned green vegetable—roasted green beans, steamed broccoli, or wilted greens—fills out the plate. Because the main course is so easy to make, you can spend a few extra moments assembling the banana-split tartlets for dessert.

A no-brainer! Any fruity, full-bodied red will work fine here. Zinfandel? Cabernet? Merlot? Choose your favorite.

PAN-SEARED STRIP STEAKS
WITH RED-WINE ONION SAUCE

For the ultimate beef experience, buy USDA prime-grade steaks from a butcher who ages the beef.

- 2 New York strip steaks (about 8 ounces each)
  Fresh-ground black pepper
- 1 tablespoon cooking oil
- 1½ tablespoons butter
- ½ small red onion, cut into thin slices
- ¼ cup red wine, such as Côtes-du-Rhône
- ½ cup plus 1 tablespoon beef stock or canned low-sodium beef broth
- ½ teaspoon arrowroot
  Salt
- 1 tablespoon minced flat-leaf parsley

1. Heat the oven to 200°. Sprinkle both sides of the steaks with pepper.

2. In a large, heavy, stainless-steel frying pan, heat the oil over high heat. When it begins to smoke, add the steaks and sear them for 2 minutes on each side. Transfer to a heatproof plate and keep warm in the oven.

3. Wipe out the pan and add the butter to it. Add the onion and cook over high heat, stirring, until browned, 2 to 3 minutes. Add the wine and ½ cup of the stock and boil over moderately high heat until the liquid is reduced to ¼ cup, about 4 minutes.

4. Dissolve the arrowroot in the remaining 1 tablespoon of stock and stir into the sauce. Remove the pan from the heat, add the steak juices from the plate, and season with salt and pepper. Sprinkle the steaks with the parsley and serve at once on warmed plates with the onion sauce.

—BOB CHAMBERS

MASHED YUKON GOLDS WITH BUTTERMILK

For a hint of garlic, add one peeled garlic clove to the cooking water and work it through the ricer along with the potatoes.

1¼ pounds Yukon Gold potatoes, peeled and quartered
    Salt
⅓ cup buttermilk
2 tablespoons butter
2 tablespoons minced fresh chives or scallion tops
    Fresh-ground black pepper

In a large saucepan, cover the potatoes with cold water and add 1 teaspoon salt. Boil over high heat until tender, 15 to 18 minutes. Drain, reserving 2 or 3 tablespoons of the cooking liquid. Pass the potatoes through a ricer or food mill set over the pan. Stir in the buttermilk, butter, and chives. Season with salt and pepper. Add the reserved cooking liquid to desired consistency and rewarm over moderately low heat before serving.

—BOB CHAMBERS

GAME PLAN

Make the tartlets and freeze.

Boil the potatoes.

Prepare the green vegetable.

Sear the steaks and make the onion sauce.

Mash the potatoes.

BANANA-SPLIT TARTLETS

An easy crust made of vanilla-cookie crumbs and melted butter makes quick work of these tartlets.

⅔ cup vanilla-cookie crumbs
    Dash cinnamon
2 tablespoons plus 1 teaspoon unsalted butter
2 tablespoons sugar
2 tablespoons water
¼ cup semisweet chocolate chips
¼ teaspoon vanilla extract
2 tablespoons sweetened coconut flakes
2 tablespoons sliced almonds
    Vanilla ice cream
1 small ripe banana, cut into thin slices

1. Heat the oven to 350°. In a bowl, combine the cookie crumbs and cinnamon. Melt the 2 tablespoons of butter and add to the bowl. Blend lightly with your fingers. Press the crumbs into two 3-inch tartlet pans and bake for about 5 minutes, until golden. Let cool.

2. In a small saucepan, combine the sugar and water and bring to a boil. Remove from the heat; stir in the chocolate chips and the remaining 1 teaspoon butter until melted. Stir in the vanilla and set aside to cool.

3. On a baking sheet, toast the coconut and almonds for about 5 minutes, or until golden.

4. Place a scoop of ice cream in each tartlet shell and drizzle with some of the chocolate sauce. Top with the sliced banana and sprinkle with the coconut and almonds. Spoon some chocolate sauce over all. Chill in the freezer.

5. Serve the tartlets with the remaining sauce on the side.

—BOB CHAMBERS

CHICKEN RUMBA

I n the American South, chicken is called the gospel bird because of its place on the Sunday dinner table, but cooks everywhere are equally thankful for chicken's versatility and ease of preparation for weeknight meals. This dinner blends flavors from the American South and the Caribbean, and at its heart are chicken breasts glazed with a lively mango rum sauce. Dilled green beans turn up with crisp oven-fried slices of sweet potato. For dessert, we suggest a store-bought pecan pie.

Sémillon, long established in France and a regular in Australia, is catching on in the Pacific Northwest. Examples from Oregon (and Australia) are soft, fruity, and silky in the mouth, making a good match with the glazed chicken.

ROAST CHICKEN WITH MANGO RUM GLAZE

A glaze of mango nectar and mango chutney, available in supermarkets, adds sweet fruitiness to chicken. Serve with lemon wedges as a counterpoint, if you like.

    A mixture of ¼ teaspoon dried thyme, ⅛ teaspoon dried, rubbed sage, and ⅛ teaspoon ground allspice
- ½ teaspoon salt
- ¼ teaspoon fresh-ground black pepper
- 2 boneless, skinless chicken breasts (about 5 ounces each)
- 1½ teaspoons olive oil
- ¼ cup bottled mango chutney
- ¼ cup canned mango nectar or fresh orange juice
- 2 tablespoons rum, preferably dark

1. Heat the oven to 500°. In a small bowl, combine the poultry seasoning, salt, and pepper. Rub the chicken with the oil and then the dry seasoning. Cover and refrigerate for at least 20 minutes or for up to 2 hours.

2. Set the chicken breasts, skinned-side up, in an oiled baking dish, and roast for 15 minutes.

3. Meanwhile, in a food processor or blender, puree the chutney, mango nectar, and rum. Brush the chicken with 2 tablespoons of the mango glaze and bake for about 10 minutes, until browned and cooked through. Transfer the chicken to plates and serve with the remaining glaze.

—JESSICA B. HARRIS

variation: Roast Pork with Mango Rum Glaze
Rub one pork tenderloin or two thick pork loin chops with oil and the dry seasonings. Cover with plastic wrap and refrigerate for at least 20 minutes or for up to 2 hours. Set the meat in an oiled baking dish and roast, turning twice, for 10 minutes. Brush the tenderloin with 2 or 3 tablespoons of the mango glaze. Roast until the meat is browned and an instant-read thermometer inserted in the thickest part registers 150°. Let rest for 5 minutes before cutting into six slices. Serve with the remaining mango glaze.

SWEET-POTATO CHIPS

2 medium sweet potatoes, peeled and cut into ¼-inch slices
1 tablespoon cooking oil
  Salt and fresh-ground black pepper

Heat the oven to 375°. Line a large rimmed baking sheet with parchment paper. Toss the sweet potato slices with the oil on the prepared baking sheet. Season generously with salt and pepper and toss once again. Roast for about 20 minutes, turning occasionally, until tender and lightly browned. (*The chips can stand at room temperature for up to 3 hours; recrisp in a 500° oven before serving.*)

—JESSICA B. HARRIS

GAME PLAN

Rub the chicken with the seasonings and let marinate.

Heat the oven to 375°.

Bake the sweet-potato chips. Remove them from the oven and raise the heat to 500°.

Bake the chicken.

Cook the green beans and toss with the dill and lemon.

Rewarm the sweet-potato chips at the last minute.

DILLED GREEN BEANS

½ pound green beans, stems removed
1 tablespoon butter
1 teaspoon minced fresh dill
1½ teaspoons lemon juice
    Salt and fresh-ground black pepper

1. Bring a stainless-steel saucepan of salted water to a boil. Add the beans and cook over moderate heat until crisp-tender, about 5 minutes; drain.

2. Melt the butter in the saucepan. Add the beans and dill and sauté over moderately high heat until tender, about 5 minutes. Sprinkle with the lemon juice, season with salt and pepper, and serve.

—JESSICA B. HARRIS

COD ROAST

B aking fish and potatoes together is an old tradition, and all too often the technique yields undercooked potatoes and overcooked fish. The brilliance of tonight's recipe is that the potatoes are baked for twenty-five minutes without the fish; then the cod is set on top to roast for about ten minutes. The result is tender, browned potatoes with perfectly done fish. A salad of baby greens with a Parmesan-cheese dressing is the ideal accompaniment. Warm, nutty caramel sauce over vanilla ice cream concludes the meal.

Vernaccia di San Gimignano—medium-bodied, refreshing, with a pleasantly bitter finish—is a great choice. For additional character in the wine, look for Terre di Tufi, an oaked version of vernaccia from Terruzzi & Puthod.

ROASTED COD WITH POTATOES AND LEEKS
To save cooking time, use a food processor or mandoline to slice the potatoes very thin.

2½ tablespoons butter
2   medium leeks, white and light-green parts only, chopped and rinsed well
1   cup sliced mushrooms
    Salt and fresh-ground black pepper
1   tablespoon chopped flat-leaf parsley
¾   pound red potatoes, peeled and sliced thin
¾   cup chicken stock or canned low-sodium chicken broth
¾   pound cod fillet, in one piece
1   teaspoon olive oil
1   plum tomato, diced

1. Heat the oven to 450°. In a large frying pan, melt 1 tablespoon of the butter. Add the leeks and cook over moderately high heat, stirring, until softened, 2 to 3 minutes. Add the mushrooms, season with salt and pepper, and cook, stirring, until the vegetables are tender and the juices have evaporated, about 5 minutes. Stir in 2 teaspoons of the parsley and remove from the heat.

2. Coat an 8-inch-square baking pan with 1 tablespoon butter. Layer one-third of the potatoes in the pan, overlapping slightly; sprinkle with salt and pepper. Spoon half of the leek mixture over the potatoes, top with another layer of potatoes, and season with salt and pepper. Repeat with the remaining leeks and potatoes. Sprinkle with salt and pepper, dot with the remaining ½ tablespoon butter, and pour the stock around the edges. Bake in the upper third of the oven for 25 minutes, or until the potatoes are tender. If they start to overbrown, cover loosely with aluminum foil.

3. Rub the cod with the oil, season with salt and pepper, and set it on the potatoes. Scatter the tomato and the remaining 1 teaspoon parsley over the fish. Bake, uncovered, for 8 to 10 minutes, or until the cod is cooked through. Serve immediately, spooning any pan juices over the potatoes.

—JUDITH SUTTON

GAME PLAN

Heat the oven.

Toast the nuts for the caramel sauce while the oven heats.

Prepare and bake the vegetables for the fish dish.

Add the fish to the vegetables.

Make the caramel sauce.

Toss the salad.

MIXED BABY GREENS WITH PARMESAN DRESSING

½ clove garlic
2 teaspoons grated Parmesan
2 teaspoons wine vinegar
1 teaspoon balsamic vinegar
Pinch dried oregano
Salt and fresh-ground black pepper
1½ tablespoons olive oil
¼ pound mixed baby greens
1 tablespoon pine nuts

In a mini-processor, combine the garlic, Parmesan, wine vinegar, balsamic vinegar, oregano and salt and pepper to taste and process until smooth. With the machine on, add the oil in a steady stream and process until smooth. Transfer to a bowl, add the mixed greens and pine nuts, and toss.

—Susan Shapiro Jaslove

WALNUT CARAMEL SUNDAES

Heat the cream while the caramel cooks so that it can be added when the caramel is removed from the heat; otherwise the sauce may burn.

⅓ cup walnut halves
¼ cup sugar
2 tablespoons water
¼ cup heavy cream
Pinch salt
Vanilla ice cream

1. Heat the oven to 400°. Spread the walnuts on a baking sheet and toast for about 5 minutes, or until fragrant. Chop the nuts.

2. In a heavy medium saucepan, combine the sugar with the water. Bring to a boil over moderately high heat. Cook without stirring until the sugar turns a rich, tea-like brown, about 7 minutes. Immediately remove from the heat.

3. Meanwhile, in a small saucepan, bring the cream and salt just to a boil over moderate heat. Slowly pour the cream into the caramel and stir gently until combined; be careful because the caramel may spatter. Stir in the toasted walnuts, let cool slightly, and serve. Or reheat gently when ready to serve.

4. Scoop vanilla ice cream into two tall glasses or small bowls. Spoon the walnut caramel sauce on top.

—Bob Chambers

A JUICY ROAST

A roasted pork loin on the bone is an excellent midweek choice for dinner. It is easy to prepare and a nice change from the familiar boneless loin; plus it provides leftovers for sandwiches the following day. Serve the succulent pork with braised cabbage and apples and steamed red potatoes. Dessert is pure comfort: The maple bread pudding tastes like a cross between crème brûlée and French toast.

Tocai friulano is a fruity and refreshing variety of white wine from northeast Italy and largely unknown here in the United States. Well-made examples have melon and mineral aromas and flavors. If tough to find, substitute a high-quality pinot grigio.

ROASTED PORK LOIN WITH GARLIC
Asking the butcher to remove the chine bone from the pork loin makes for easy carving.

3 pounds center-cut pork loin roast, chine bone removed
3 cloves garlic, cut into thin slices
  Salt and fresh-ground black pepper
1 tablespoon cooking oil

1. Heat the oven to 425°. Using a small knife, cut deep slits all over the pork and insert a sliver of garlic into each one. Sprinkle the loin on both sides with salt and pepper.

2. In a small roasting pan, heat the oil. Add the pork loin and cook over moderately high heat, turning occasionally, until nicely browned all over, about 5 minutes. Insert a meat thermometer in the center of the pork, making sure it does not touch the bone.

Transfer the pan to the oven and roast the pork for about 50 minutes, or until the internal temperature reaches 150°. Transfer to a carving board and let stand for 10 minutes. Carve the pork into ½-inch-thick slices.

—STEPHANIE LYNESS

BRAISED CABBAGE WITH APPLES

To add even more flavor to the cabbage, stir in the degreased pan juices from the pork just before serving.

⅛ teaspoon ground coriander
1 tablespoon olive oil
1 medium onion, cut into thin slices
1 Golden Delicious apple, cut into thin slices
½ teaspoon salt
1 pound shredded green cabbage (about 4 cups)
¼ cup dry white wine
¼ cup chicken stock or canned low-sodium chicken broth
2 tablespoons cider vinegar
Fresh-ground black pepper

1. In a large frying pan, toast the coriander over moderate heat, stirring, until fragrant, about 1 minute. Transfer to a small bowl.

2. Heat the oil in the pan. Add the onion, apple, and ¼ teaspoon of the salt. Cover and cook, stirring occasionally, over moderately low heat until the onion is translucent, about 5 minutes. Stir in the shredded cabbage, toasted coriander, wine, stock, vinegar, and the remaining ¼ teaspoon salt. Bring to a boil. Cover and simmer over low heat until the cabbage is tender, about 20 minutes. Season with pepper and more salt if needed.

—STEPHANIE LYNESS

MAPLE BOURBON BREAD PUDDING

2 slices whole wheat bread, crusts removed
2 slices firm white bread, crusts removed
2 large egg yolks

GAME PLAN

Heat the oven to 425°.

Assemble the bread puddings.

Roast the pork.

Start the cabbage and cook the potatoes.

Remove the pork from the oven and lower the temperature to 325°.

Bake the puddings.

3 tablespoons maple syrup, plus more for drizzling
1 tablespoon bourbon (optional)
¾ cup heavy cream

1. Heat the oven to 350°. Lightly butter two 8-ounce ramekins or custard cups. Cut the whole wheat and white bread into ½-inch cubes, spread on a baking sheet, and toast in the oven for 10 minutes. Divide the bread cubes between the two ramekins. Reduce the oven temperature to 325°.

2. In a bowl, whisk together the egg yolks, maple syrup, and bourbon, if using. In a small saucepan, warm the cream until just hot to the touch. Whisk the cream into the egg mixture and strain over the bread cubes. Press plastic wrap directly onto the bread so that all of it is completely submerged in the custard. Let stand at room temperature until the bread is completely soaked, about 10 minutes.

3. Remove the plastic wrap; cover the ramekins with aluminum foil. Set them in a larger baking dish and pour water into the dish to reach halfway up the side of the ramekins. Bake for about 30 minutes, or until the custard is just set. Let cool briefly, drizzle with warm maple syrup, and serve.

—Larry Hayden

SAGE SCENTS

The kitchen always smells good when you cook with sage. The herb's distinctive resinous quality is a natural for cold-weather dishes made with pork (or poultry or veal). The menu here pairs pork medallions—cut from the tenderloin—with an easy pan sauce flavored with balsamic vinegar as well as sage. A creamy fennel gratin, a bay-scented pilaf, and a simple green salad round out the main course. After such a satisfying meal, fresh fruit is all that is needed for dessert.

Pinotage, a South African exclusive, is a cross between pinot noir and cinsault. The result is a wine of good color, soft structure, spice, and sometimes smoky tones, which will echo the balsamic vinegar and sage. Nederburg and Kanonkop are good brands.

SAUTÉED PORK MEDALLIONS WITH BALSAMIC VINEGAR AND SAGE

Do not cook the pork medallions much past medium rare (160°); they will be dry and less flavorful if sautéed too long.

1 pork tenderloin (about ¾ pound), trimmed
1 tablespoon flour
  Salt and fresh-ground black pepper
1 teaspoon butter
2 teaspoons olive oil
⅓ cup balsamic vinegar
2 tablespoons chicken stock or canned low-sodium chicken broth
1½ teaspoons chopped fresh sage

1. Cut the tenderloin on a slight angle into four 1¼-inch medallions. Pound them lightly with the flat side of a large knife to flatten. On a plate, season the flour with salt and pepper. Dredge the medallions in the seasoned flour and shake off the excess.

2. In a large stainless-steel frying pan, melt the butter with the oil over moderately high heat. Add the medallions and cook until nicely browned on the outside and medium rare on the inside, 2 to 3 minutes per side. Transfer to a plate, cover with aluminum foil, and keep warm.

3. Drain the fat from the pan. Add the vinegar and simmer, scraping the bottom of the pan with a wooden spoon to dislodge any brown bits, until the mixture is thickened and reduced by about half. Add the stock and any accumulated juices from the pork; boil until reduced to a dark, shiny sauce, about 1 minute. Add the sage and season to taste with salt and pepper. Arrange the medallions on two plates and spoon the sauce on top.

—STEPHANIE LYNESS

FENNEL GRATIN

If you wish to subtly highlight the anise notes of fennel, stir one-quarter teaspoon (and not a drop more) of Pernod or other anise-flavored spirit into the cream before pouring over the fennel.

1 to 2 bulbs fennel (about 1 pound), trimmed, quartered, and cut
    lengthwise into thin slices
¼ teaspoon salt
⅛ teaspoon fresh-ground black pepper
¾ cup heavy cream
2 tablespoons dry bread crumbs
2 tablespoons grated Parmesan
2 teaspoons butter

1. Heat the oven to 425°. Butter a small gratin or other shallow baking dish. Arrange the fennel slices in the dish. In a small bowl, whisk the salt and pepper into the cream and pour over the fennel. Sprinkle on the bread crumbs and then the Parmesan. Dot with the butter.

GAME PLAN

Heat the oven.

Make the fennel gratin and bake.

Start the pilaf.

Assemble a green salad.

Cook the pork and make the pan sauce.

2. Cover the gratin with aluminum foil and bake for 20 minutes. Remove the foil and continue baking the gratin for about 15 minutes longer, until the cream has reduced and the top is browned.

—STEPHANIE LYNESS

RICE PILAF WITH BAY LEAF

Adding a bay leaf to stocks and soups is almost automatic, but we often neglect this flavorful herb in other dishes. Here, it lends an intense fragrance to a pilaf.

1½ cups chicken stock or canned low-sodium chicken broth
  1 tablespoon butter
  1 small onion, chopped
 ¾ cup arborio rice
  1 bay leaf
 ¼ teaspoon salt
   Fresh-ground white pepper

1. In a medium saucepan, bring the stock to a simmer over moderate heat.

2. Meanwhile, in a medium frying pan, melt the butter over moderate heat. Add the onion and cook, stirring, for 2 minutes. Stir in the rice and bay leaf; cook until the onion is soft and the rice is translucent, about 5 minutes. Add the hot stock and the salt to the frying pan. Reduce the heat to low, cover and simmer gently until the liquid is absorbed and the rice is tender but still firm in the center, 18 to 20 minutes. Discard the bay leaf. Season the rice with white pepper to taste and serve hot.

—STEPHANIE LYNESS

SPICED LAMB CHOPS

Coriander, cumin, cinnamon, and cloves—the four big Cs of your spice shelf provide a North African approach to these lamb loin chops. The remarkably easy panfry is served over couscous with a side dish of spinach, golden raisins, and pine nuts. For dessert, the oranges and amaretto continue the Mediterranean theme.

The spices here are nicely echoed by a powerful red Burgundy, such as a Gevrey-Chambertin or an Echézeaux. A less expensive option would be a spicy California zinfandel.

SPICED LAMB CHOPS WITH COUSCOUS

Searing the lamb chops on the stovetop and finishing the cooking in the oven ensures tender succulent meat.

- 1 teaspoon ground coriander
- 1 teaspoon ground cinnamon
- 1 teaspoon ground cumin
- ¼ teaspoon ground cloves
- ¾ teaspoon salt
- 1 teaspoon fresh-ground black pepper
- 4 lamb loin chops, about ¾ inch thick
- 1 tablespoon olive oil
- 1 cup water
- 1 teaspoon butter
- ⅔ cup couscous

1. In a small bowl, combine the coriander, cinnamon, cumin, cloves, ½ teaspoon of the salt, and the pepper. Coat the lamb on both sides with the spice mixture. Heat the oven to 400°.

2. Heat the oil in a large frying pan. Add the lamb chops and sear over high heat, turning the chops once, until browned, 2 to 3 minutes per side. Transfer the chops to a rimmed baking sheet; reserve the pan juices.

3. In a small saucepan, bring the water to a boil with the butter and the remaining ¼ teaspoon salt. Stir in the couscous. Cover, remove from the heat, and let stand for 5 minutes. Set aside in a warm place.

4. Bake the lamb chops for about 10 minutes, or until firm to the touch. Fluff the couscous with a fork. Divide between two plates, set the lamb chops on top, and spoon any pan juices over.

—PEGGY RYAN

SPINACH WITH PINE NUTS

  2 tablespoons golden raisins
1½ teaspoons olive oil
  ¾ pound spinach, stems removed and leaves washed
  1 tablespoon pine nuts
    Salt and fresh-ground black pepper

1. In a small bowl, cover the raisins with warm water and let stand until plumped, about 10 minutes; drain.

2. Heat the oil in a frying pan. Add the spinach, raisins, and pine nuts and cook over moderately high heat, stirring, until just wilted, about 5 minutes. Press the spinach to remove any excess liquid, season with salt and pepper, and serve.

—PEGGY RYAN

ORANGE GRATIN WITH AMARETTO SABAYON

Amaretto liqueur has the flavor of almonds, yet it is made from the kernels of apricot pits.

  2 medium navel oranges
  2 large egg yolks
2½ tablespoons sugar

GAME PLAN

Heat the oven.

Make the sabayon; segment the oranges.

Wash and stem the spinach.

Combine the spices for the lamb chops.

Cook the spinach and the lamb chops.

Broil the sabayon just before serving.

2½ tablespoons dry white wine
1 tablespoon amaretto liqueur

1. Using a sharp knife, peel the oranges, removing all of the bitter white pith. Cut in between the membranes to release the orange sections. Arrange the sections in two small gratin or shallow flameproof dishes.

2. In the top of a double boiler set over simmering water, combine the egg yolks, sugar, wine, and amaretto. Whisk constantly until thick and light, about 5 minutes. (*The sabayon can be refrigerated for up to 1 hour.*)

3. Heat the broiler. Position an oven rack about 6 inches from the heat. Spoon the sabayon over the oranges and broil for 1 minute, until browned on top.

—PEGGY RYAN

Index

Page numbers in **boldface** indicate photographs.

G

N

S

Recommended Wines

A

ALBARIÑO
  with Clams with Garlic Sauce, 45
AMARONE DELLA VALPOLICELLA
  with Fennel-and-Tomato Soup
    with Italian Sausages, 203
ARNEIS
  with Baked Fusilli with Roasted
    Vegetables, 165

B

BARBERA
  with Barbecued Chicken, 90
  with Pan-Roasted Veal Steaks, 27
BEAUJOLAIS
  with Gratinéed Ziti and Spinach, 58
BIANCO DI CUSTOZA
  with Roasted-Vegetable Tart, 99
BORDEAUX, RED
  with Filet Mignon with Shallots
    and Cognac, 61
  with Lemon Pepper Lamb Chops,
    162
BORDEAUX, WHITE
  with Chicken with Portobello
    Mushroom Sauce, 74
  with Shrimp and Avocado with
    Mustard Vinaigrette, 65
BOURGUEIL
  with Marinated-Steak Salad, 83
BOUTARI
  with Linguine with Tomato Pesto,
    93
BRUSCO DEI BARBI
  with Italian-Style Steak with Basil
    and Sage, 233
BURGUNDY, RED
  with Grilled Tuna with Rosemary
    and Thyme, 111

  with Seared-Tuna Niçoise Salad
    186
  with Spiced Lamb Chops with
    Couscous, 293
BURGUNDY, WHITE
  with Grilled Shrimp and Scallops,
    41
  with Veal Scaloppine with Lemon,
    Black Pepper, and Vermouth, 97

C

CABERNET FRANC
  with Marinated-Steak Salad, 83
CABERNET SAUVIGNON,
  CALIFORNIA
  with Filet Mignon with Shallots
    and Cognac, 61
  with Pan-Seared Strip Steaks with
    Red-Wine Onion Sauce, 275
CAHORS
  with Lamb Chops with Red Wine
    and Thyme, 257
CARNEROS PINOT NOIR
  with Grilled Tuna with Rosemary
    and Thyme, 111
CARRUADES DE LAFITE
  with Filet Mignon with Shallots
    and Cognac, 61
CAYMUS CABERNET SAUVIGNON
  with Filet Mignon with Shallots
    and Cognac, 61
CHABLIS
  with Cheddar Cheese Polenta
    with Mushroom Ragout, 173
  with Sea Bass with White Wine
    and Lemongrass, 48
  with Steamed Lobster with Lime
    Butter, 138
CHARDONNAY, AUSTRALIA
  with Ham-and-Cheese Strata, 261

  with Pork Chops with Red
    Onions, 179
  with Turkey Schnitzel, 249
CHARDONNAY, CALIFORNIA
  with Ham-and-Cheese Strata, 261
  with Pork Chops with Red
    Onions, 179
  with Pork Steaks with Ancho
    Sauce, 135
  with Turkey Schnitzel, 249
CHARDONNAY, CHILE
  with Ham-and-Cheese Strata, 261
  with Sesame Chicken in a Bun,
    205
CHARDONNAY, FRANCE
  with Ginger-Glazed Chicken, 51
  with Smoked Trout Chowder,
    245
CHARDONNAY, NEW ZEALAND
  with Fettuccine with Creamy
    Chicken and Spinach, 37
CHARDONNAY, OREGON
  with Veal Scaloppine with Lemon,
    Black Pepper, and Vermouth, 97
CHÂTEAU LAFITE-ROTHSCHILD
  with Filet Mignon with Shallots
    and Cognac, 61
CHÂTEAU LAGRAZETTE
  with Lamb Chops with Red Wine
    and Thyme, 257
CHÂTEAUNEUF-DU-PAPE
  with Panfried Quail and Italian
    Sausage, 242
CHENIN BLANC
  with Chicken Stew with
    Cornmeal Dumplings, 253
CHIANTI
  with Fennel-and-Tomato Soup
    with Italian Sausages, 203
  with Linguine with Bitter Greens
    and Pancetta, 219

Contributors

Nancy Verde Barr is a Providence-based food writer and cookbook author. She is the author of *We Called It Macaroni* (Alfred Knopf) and is currently working on *Simply Italian* (Knopf), due out this year.

Shelley Boris is a chef who lives in Garrison, New York.

Jocelyn Bulow is chef of Plouf, a seafood bistro in San Francisco, California.

Penelope Casas is a food and travel writer, cookbook author, and cooking teacher. She is currently working on *Paella Perfect* (Henry Holt), due out in the spring of 1999.

Bob Chambers is executive chef at Lancôme-L'Oréal in New York City.

Ann Clark, author of *Quick Cuisine* (Dutton), is a food writer and culinary historian from Austin, Texas.

Marcia Cone and **Thelma Snyder** are food writers and the authors of numerous microwave cookbooks, including *Home Cooking in Minutes* (Simon & Schuster).

Susan Costner is a St. Helena, California-based food writer and author of *Great Sandwiches* (Crown). Her most recent book is *Mostly Vegetables* (Bantam).

Chata DuBose is a food writer and consultant who teaches cooking classes in Houston, Texas.

Jonathan Eismann is chef/owner of Pacific Time in Miami Beach, Florida, and is currently working on a cookbook.

Amy Farges, co-owner of Harvest Imports, Inc. and Marché aux Délices, is the author of the *Aux Délices des Bois Cookbook* (Workman), due out this year.

Sarah Fritschner is the food editor of the *Courier Journal* in Louisville, Kentucky, and the author of *Vegetarian Express Lane Cookbook* (Chapters).

Paul Grimes is a chef, instructor, and food writer and stylist. He lives in New York City.

Jessica B. Harris is a Brooklyn-based cookbook author, food scholar, and culinary historian. She is currently working on *Africa: A Continent of Cuisines from Algeria to Zimbabwe* (Simon & Schuster).

Larry Hayden is a teacher, food writer, and pastry chef based in East Hampton, New York. He is author of *Sweet Success!* (Scribner), due out in the spring of 1998.

James Henahan is executive chef of Simon Pearce Restaurant in Quechee, Vermont.

Susan Shapiro Jaslove is a food writer, recipe developer, and cooking teacher based in Warren, New Jersey.

Marcia Kiesel is associate director of FOOD & WINE Magazine's test kitchen and a co-author of *Simple Art of Vietnamese Cooking* (Prentice Hall).

Johanne Killeen and **George Germon** are chefs of Al Forno in Providence, Rhode Island.

Stephanie Lyness, a food writer and cooking teacher based in Guilford, Connecticut, is the author of *Cooking with Steam* (William Morrow).

Nico Martin is a San Francisco-based chef and caterer.

Zarela Martinez is a cookbook author, food writer, and chef/owner of Zarela Restaurant in New York City. She is author of *Foods from My Heart* and *The Food and Life of Oaxaca* (both from Macmillan).

Grace Parisi is a recipe tester and developer for FOOD & WINE and author of *Summer/Winter Pasta* (Quill).

Peggy Ryan is chef/owner of Va Penseiro Restaurant in Evanston, Illinois.

Tracey Seaman is a food writer and test kitchen director from Atlantic Highlands, New Jersey. She is author of *The Tunafish Gourmet* (Villard).

Marie Simmons is an Oakland-based cookbook author, food writer, and cooking teacher. She is the author of *Rice, the Amazing Grain* (Henry Holt) and her latest book is *A to Z Pancakes* (Chapters/Houghton-Mifflin).

Diana Sturgis is FOOD & WINE Magazine's test kitchen director.

Judith Sutton is a food writer, cookbook editor, and consultant based in New York City.

Anne Walsh is a Princeton, New Jersey-based cookbook author and food writer. She is the author of *Good Food Fast* (American Express Publishing Corporation).

Kenneth Wapner is a food writer from Woodstock, New York.

John Willoughby and **Chris Schlesinger** are the co-authors of five cookbooks, including *The Thrill of the Grill* and, most recently, *License to Grill* (all William Morrow). Willoughby is a food writer and teacher, and Schlesinger is chef/owner of the East Coast Grill in Cambridge, Massachusetts.

Clifford A. Wright is a cook, food writer, and the author of *Grill Italian* (Macmillan). The California-based author's most recent book is *Italian Pure & Simple* (William Morrow).

Wayne Young is a freelance writer and the sommelier at Becco Ristorante in New York City. He studied wine at the International Wine Center and with the Wine and Spirits Education Trust.

PHOTOGRAPHERS

Elizabeth Watt: pages 12, 16, 24, 30, 44, 72, 82, 86, 94, 110, 134, 142, 154, 158, 176, 182, 196, 202, 206, 228, 232, 238, 252, 278, 290

Melanie Acevedo: pages 146, 218, 268

Mary Ellen Bartley: pages 56, 172, 188

Beatriz Da Costa: page 260

Reed Davis: page 246

Mark Ferri: pages 166, 282

Dana Gallagher: pages 38, 62

Gentl & Hyers: pages 52, 106, 212

Rita Maas: page 130

Evan Sklar: page 274

Ann Stratton: pages 100, 118, 124